HOW THE MIGHTY HAVE FALLEN

Lessons in Leadership from the Life of King Saul

-by-

Gregg T. Johnson

*How the mighty have fallen,
And the weapons of war perished!*
2 Samuel 1:27

How The Mighty Have Fallen

COPYRIGHT©2013
Gregg T. Johnson

All rights reserved. No part of this book may be reproduced, stored in a retrieval system, or transmitted in any form or by any means: electronic, mechanical, photocopy, recording, or any other (except for brief quotations in printed reviews) without the prior permission of Gregg T. Johnson

All scripture quotations are taken from
The Holy Bible, New King James Version
Copyright © 1982 by Thomas Nelson, Inc.

Cover photo of "Fallen Warrior" is on display at Glyptotek of Monaco of Bavaria, Germany. Photograph has been donated as public domain and the author has relinquished any claim to all rights in the world, including all related rights or other similar rights, as permitted by law.

Special thanks to Janet Spinelli-Dunn for
proof reading and editing

ISBN 978-0-9741036-4-8

Additional copies of this book can be purchased at
www.MissionChurch.com

Or by contacting
The Mission Church
4101 Rt. 52
Holmes NY 12531, USA

A portion of the proceeds goes to equipping
Christian Leaders around the world.

www.GreggTJohnson.com
www.GlobalLeadershipTraining.org
www.LeadershipTeachingMagazine.com

Printed in the United States by Morris Publishing®
3212 East Highway 30
Kearney, NE 68847
1-800-650-7888

How The Mighty Have Fallen

The wise profit from fools more than fools from the wise; for wise men shun the mistakes of fools, but fools copy not the wisdom of the wise.

Cato the Elder

How The Mighty Have Fallen

TABLE OF CONTENTS

Foreword from Dr. Charles Crabtree	6
A Note from Dr. Paul Frimpong Manso	7
Introduction	9
Lesson 1 Saul Was Elevated Prematurely	13
Lesson 2 Saul Usurped His Leader	29
Lesson 3 Saul Abused His Authority	43
Lesson 4 Saul Loved Man's Praise More Than God's Approval	59
Lesson 5 Saul Turned His Ministry into a Monument	77
Lesson 6 Saul Surrendered to a Spirit of Fear	89
Lesson 7 Saul Was Threatened by Other Leaders	103
Lesson 8 Saul Failed to Manage Conflict	117
Lesson 9 Saul Lacked Integrity	135
Lesson 10 Saul Destroyed Himself	153
A Final Word	178
Endnotes	184
About the Author	186

FOREWORD

Because of the twenty-five years I have spent in national leadership and more recently as president of a Bible college dealing with ministries and those in training for ministry, I have read many books on the subject of the rise, fall, and restoration of ministers. *How The Mighty Have Fallen*, by Gregg T. Johnson, is the best I have read on the subject.

In using the life of King Saul as an example of all the pitfalls facing a charismatic leader, Gregg Johnson identifies the inevitable temptations facing all leaders connect to the Kingdom God.

The reader of *How The Mighty Have Fallen* will not only see the path to ultimate disgrace but most importantly, the road to ultimate restoration and victory. The book is a great read about Saul, but it holds up a mission to the reader.

Dr. Charles T. Crabtree

President, Zion Bible College (Northpoint College)
Former Assistant General Superintendent,
Assemblies of God, USA

A NOTE FROM
REV. DR. PAUL FRIMPONG MANSO

"How the Mighty Have Fallen," is very crucial and relevant in our day and time; a must read for all, especially practicing leaders at every level of leadership.

In this book, Gregg Johnson addresses character flaws in leaders and how, if they are left unattended to at the very early stages of one's life, can lead to a great down fall when one attains higher heights in leadership.

Furthermore, this book raises issues like the dangers in seeking early or premature promotion, the abuse of authority and the insecurity many leaders exhibit which leads to leadership crises. Saul is a very good character study on this subject matter and Pastor Gregg has done an excellent exposition on him. The issues raised in this book are a check list for all leaders to help us avoid wrecking our lives and the destinies of the people we lead.

I have read many books on leadership whiles serving the Lord in many leadership positions. This book is excellent and will equip the reader to walk in integrity. I also recommend it as a text book for Bible Schools and all institutions that train leaders.

- Rev. Dr. Paul Frimpong Manso
General Superintendent, Ghana Assemblies of God

How The Mighty Have Fallen

Then David lamented with this lamentation over Saul and over Jonathan his son, and he told them to teach the children of Judah the Song of the Bow; indeed it is written in the Book of Jasher: "The beauty of Israel is slain on your high places! How the mighty have fallen! Tell it not in Gath, Proclaim it not in the streets of Ashkelon— Lest the daughters of the Philistines rejoice, Lest the daughters of the uncircumcised triumph. "O mountains of Gilboa, Let there be no dew nor rain upon you, Nor fields of offerings. For the shield of the mighty is cast away there! The shield of Saul, not anointed with oil. From the blood of the slain, From the fat of the mighty, The bow of Jonathan did not turn back, And the sword of Saul did not return empty. "Saul and Jonathan were beloved and pleasant in their lives, And in their death they were not divided; They were swifter than eagles, They were stronger than lions. "O daughters of Israel, weep over Saul, Who clothed you in scarlet, with luxury; Who put ornaments of gold on your apparel. "How the mighty have fallen in the midst of the battle! Jonathan was slain in your high places. I am distressed for you, my brother Jonathan; You have been very pleasant to me; Your love to me was wonderful, Surpassing the love of women. "How the mighty have fallen, And the weapons of war perished!"

2 Samuel 1:17-27

INTRODUCTION

It was concerning King Saul that David said, "How the mighty have fallen, and the weapons of war perished" (2 Samuel 1:27). His was a life that began with great promise and celebration, but ended in miserable failure and humiliation. His life is an example of how the mightiest of leaders fail.

Why do great men and women fall? How do leaders, quick to ascend with such promise of unparalleled success, find themselves awash in disastrous failure and disgrace? More importantly, can the path toward one's downfall be discerned before it's too late and be avoided?

It is the premise of this book that such a decline can be detected and reversed. In fact, God's Word is replete with examples of great men with incredible potential who fell in ruin—for our instruction. Case study after case study is provided for our learning; it's a treasury of lessons in "what not to do." If we will apply our hearts toward understanding and recognize the patterns in their lives, we can see the dangers in our own and prevent our own demise.

Failure is a great teacher, but only if we're willing to learn from it. Mistakes are precious mentors, but only for the humble who seek to be taught rather than shifting the blame. Some of the greatest lessons we learn in life come from our past failures and mistakes. Even more, much of the wisdom we gain can be learned by watching the mistakes of others and learning "what not to do."

I still remember some of the most important lessons I learned by observing the serious blunders of leaders which led to their downfall. Two out of three pastors I served under fell into sexual sin with women in the church and destroyed their families and ministries. Painful to witness, but invaluable learning. I learned the value of maintaining sexual purity in ministry and staying close to my wife. I remember another pastor whose preaching was dry and unctionless and forced the church into decline. Difficult to sit under, but priceless lessons learned. It forced me to realize how vital it is to bring a fresh word from God, to maintain a vibrant prayer life and seek God for His anointing. I recall another who failed to provide vision to the church which invoked a culture of apathy and lukewarmness upon a people who once were on fire for God. Still, this experience provokes me to impart vision to my people and challenge them to achieve great things for Christ.

Indeed failure and mistakes, if we will learn from them, can teach us lessons to last a lifetime. So it is with King Saul. From a hopeful beginning to a miserable end, his life serves as a classroom for the studious leader. The topic of study: "Lessons in What 'Not' to Do!" By chronicling Saul's leadership career, we find contained in his mistakes valuable principles of leadership and examples of why men and women should lead with integrity. By his demise, he gives us a valuable example of what happens when leaders cast off restraint and live only for themselves. He shows us why we must be men and women of character, virtue, and humility.

This is the essence of Saul's failures. His mistakes were not methodical, organizational, or managerial. They were failures of character. His incompetence as a leader was not due to lapses in strategic planning or poor administrative skills, he failed because he was toxic. When it came to matters of integrity, and personal qualities of credible leadership, Saul was deficient and his lack of character contaminated his entire organization. Sure, he had the looks and the charisma, he had certain skills and could throw a spear, but the essential qualities of credible leadership, selflessness, courage, contrition and more—the core values that drive, motivate, and sustain a leader—had yet to be seen. In fact, when the pressures of leadership presented, Saul's lack of character would crumble and turn him into a corrupt tyrant abusing his position for personal gain.

As we approach the story of Saul, let us not do so with a critical or condescending heart. Saul was only human, just as we are human. He was thrust into a role by the will of man before God had adequately prepared him and, because of that, could not cope with the extreme pressures he faced. And let us remember that Saul is also the story of us. There is a Saul in each of us. This is why God has given us this example—so we could look into ourselves, see him, and be warned. For if we do not seek to be taught, to learn the proper way of leadership, we will come to an end not much different than the mighty man who had fallen so hard.

Then all the elders of Israel gathered together and came to Samuel at Ramah, and said to him, "Look, you are old, and your sons do not walk in your ways. Now make us a king to judge us like all the nations." ... So Samuel prayed to the LORD. And the LORD said to Samuel, "Heed the voice of the people in all that they say to you; for they have not rejected you, but they have rejected Me, that I should not reign over them."

1 Samuel 8:4-7

There was a man of Benjamin whose name was Kish...And he had a choice and handsome son whose name was Saul. There was not a more handsome person than he among the children of Israel. From his shoulders upward he was taller than any of the people.

1 Samuel 9:1-2

So they ran and brought him from there; and when he stood among the people, he was taller than any of the people from his shoulders upward. And Samuel said to all the people, "Do you see him whom the LORD has chosen, that there is no one like him among all the people?" So all the people shouted and said, "Long live the king!"

1 Samuel 10:23-24

LESSON ONE

SAUL WAS ELEVATED PREMATURELY

"The worst thing that can happen to a man is for him to succeed before he is ready."
Dr. Martin Lloyd Jones

"Give us king!" demanded Israel. They had enough of prophets and priests waiting for a word from God. They wanted a man to lead them, someone with talent, someone with leadership skills and a certain "king-like" flare. They wanted Saul.

But Saul was not what God wanted for Israel. Through Samuel, He warned the nation what would happen if the son of Kish sat on the throne. But still, the people demanded a king; and sadly, God gave them what they wanted.

It begs the question: Does God place people in leadership before it is His perfect timing to do so? Will God anoint someone even though their character has not been prepared to support that anointing? Unfortunately, it happens all the time. Both history and scripture are filled with examples of those who, despite lack of preparation or maturity, were elevated prematurely and, consequently, were ruined by that promotion.

It is not that promotion is a bad thing or that advancement in leadership should be avoided. Promotion is bad only when it puts one into a position before his character has been equipped to support that promotion. It is like trying to build a tower on a weak foundation. If the concrete hasn't been correctly mixed and fitted with rebar, it cannot support the structure and will fail under the weight of its own enlargement. In every leader's career, promotion and advancement always bring greater temptations, harsher trials, and fiercer attacks. Those who lack the character to withstand such pressure will fall and bring devastation to their lives and the Kingdom of God.

This is a truth the enemy knows very well. Too often, if the devil can't stop good men from pursuing God's call to leadership, he will try to promote them too quickly—before they are ready. He will lure them into positions that appeal to their ambition and gratify their ego, but will be laced with hidden evils they are not prepared to resist.

In Saul's promotion there were several factors at work that facilitated his premature ascent: the enamor of anointing, the lure of charisma, the cry of the crowd, and the pride of the heart. While the presence of all three collaborated in Israel's rebellion against God, it takes only one to set us in opposition to the Lord's will for our lives.

THE ENAMOR OF ANOINTING

The people made an assumption about Saul. Undoubtedly they supposed that because he was anointed by God (1 Samuel

10:1), he must be credible, trustworthy, honorable, and pure. If he wasn't good, then God wouldn't anoint him. So let's give him a crown, sit him on a throne and bow to his authority. Big mistake.

Unfortunately when it comes to the "anointing," we have a similar problem in Charismatic circles. We are easily and overly impressed by anointing. We love Spirit-empowered ministry. We love great preaching, dynamic prophesies, inspirational singing, and the Gifts of the Spirit. In fact, every couple of years we see multitudes of the enamored scurry across the country chasing after the next great anointing. They come from around the world. Stadiums fill to capacity and cameras broadcast live via satellite. As crowds cheer and people are saved and healed, the "man with the anointing" is elevated to celebrity status as God's chosen prophet of power for the hour. Simon Magnus, eat your heart out.

But what is the "anointing"?

Simply stated, the "anointing" is nothing more than God putting His hand upon someone or something and using them to fulfill His purpose at a given time. It implies no validation of character or proof of credibility except that God willed to use it. In fact, God has been known to anoint some rather dubious things despite their questionable character.

He anointed a donkey and made it preach. Balaam was anointed and he had Moab in his heart. Samson was anointed and fornicated with Philistines. Judas was anointed while he was stealing money from Jesus' purse. Caiaphas was anointed to prophesy while plotting the crucifixion. Even the rocks can be anointed to cry out if God so desires.

It's sad to say, but the longer I live, the less impressed I am with the anointing. What I'm more impressed with is character. Why? Because more and more, we are seeing gifted, talented, anointed leaders who, because of their "anointing," are promoted beyond what their character can sustain.

Proverbs 18:16 says *"a man's gift will make room for him."* It's true, if you have gift, if you can sing, preach, prophesy, or heal the sick, we'll make room for you. Like Saul, your anointing will take you right to the top. Unfortunately, what Andy Stanley said is true: *"Leaders get into trouble when their integrity doesn't keep pace with the momentum created by their giftedness."* And today we are seeing too many who, because of their anointing, are being promoted beyond what their character can sustain.

With advancement, enlargement, and promotion in the Kingdom of God comes fiercer temptations, harsher attacks, and greater opportunities for destruction. An old saying tells us, "With higher levels come higher devils" and it is possible to be promoted before one's character has been prepared to handle the kind of attacks that come at higher levels of authority and anointing. Leadership will destroy the man whose character has not been prepared for it.

Success brings enlargement. This means financial increase, more attention from enamored crowds, and more attraction from the adoring opposite sex. If one has not been conditioned for this level of temptation and attack, he is likely to fall prey to pressures when, not if, they come. Jeremiah 12:5 said it like this: *"If you have run with the footmen, and they have wearied you, then how can you contend with horses? And if in the land of peace, in which you trusted, they wearied you, then how will you do in the floodplain of the Jordan?"*

Let us be clear: the anointing of God is an essential element of ministry and leadership in the Kingdom of God. In reality, it can never be undervalued or overrated. Without anointing, preaching is reduced to a cold, dry lecture without the fire to stir men's hearts. Without anointing, worship music is merely an exhibition of human talent meant to impress the flesh. Without anointing, churches resort to stale liturgy and religious rituals lacking the capacity to transform lost, carnal souls into passionate disciples of Jesus Christ. Let us make no mistake about it: we need the anointing of God!

But in our zeal for anointing, let us not discard discernment. Just because someone is anointed does not mean he or she is trustworthy, credible, honorable or pure. Pentecostals need to know that if a person has a healing gift or a prophetic anointing, it does not necessarily mean that he or she has strong character and has been endorsed by God.

Let us remember the words of Christ on this matter in Matthew 7:15-23: *"Beware of false prophets, who come to you in sheep's clothing, but inwardly they are ravenous wolves. You will know them by their fruits. Do men gather grapes from thornbushes or figs from thistles? Even so, every good tree bears good fruit, but a bad tree bears bad fruit. A good tree cannot bear bad fruit, nor can a bad tree bear good fruit. Every tree that does not bear good fruit is cut down and thrown into the fire. Therefore by their fruits you will know them. Not everyone who says to Me, 'Lord, Lord,' shall enter the kingdom of heaven, but he who does the will of My Father in heaven. Many will say to Me in that day, 'Lord, Lord, have we not prophesied in Your name, cast out demons in Your name, and done many wonders in Your name?' And then I will declare to them, 'I never knew you; depart from Me, you who practice lawlessness!'"*

Clearly, Jesus was more impressed with character than He

was with anointing. We should be as well.

THE LURE OF CHARISMA

Saul was promoted for one reason: he looked good. Scripture describes him as being "choice and handsome" and "there was not a more handsome person than he among the children of Israel. From his shoulders upward he was taller than any of the people." Israel wanted a king who had strong outward appeal who could legitimize them before other nations. Sadly, God gave them what they wanted: a king whose only good quality was how he looked on the outside.

Israel's infatuation with Saul betrays a disturbing truth of what humanity often values in leadership. More often, we admire leaders for their charisma and style rather than their character and substance.

Charisma is about persona and magnetism. It's the ability to charm others and win their affections. Charismatic leaders are gregarious and enthusiastic. They have a way of inspiring and exciting people and giving them a positive sense about themselves. Their affect has nothing to do with moral capacity; it has only to do with the good feelings they impart to those around them. This is why charismatic people draw crowds, have popular appeal, become famous and win elections. Outwardly, they are attractive. Inwardly, however, can be a very different story.

And then there's style. We love "stylish" leaders. It's all about looks and presentation; it's being fashionable and in vogue. A stylish person is impressive, not because of intelligence or integrity, but because of a certain panache that appeals to the carnal senses.

Saul had it all. He was young, so he was in vogue. He was handsome and emitted that certain charisma. In the eyes of men, he was the obvious choice. Unfortunately, it was that irresistible charm that fostered his premature promotion and, eventually, his downfall.

We see it all the time—charismatic leaders whose stylish persona has elevated them beyond what their character can support. Several years ago, a nationally renowned TV bishop told his wife, "Today God had shown me the woman I was supposed to have married." Within a month of their divorce he married his new girlfriend. Even more recent, the leader of a national fellowship of thirty million evangelical members confessed to sexual immorality, homosexual relations, and illegal drug use. Then there was the national evangelist and famous speaker of men's conferences who was arrested for use of child pornography and convicted. In 2010, a famous televangelist, mega-church pastor and international "Christian celebrity" was accused and sued by four young men in his mentorship program of homosexual coercion. Many still remember the "healing revival" in Florida which drew international attention to the flamboyant "healing evangelist" who led it. Within months the evangelist was discovered to be involved in an "inappropriate" relationship with a female member of his staff. He has since divorced his wife, married his girlfriend, and has restarted his ministry.

Character? Integrity? Ethics? These don't really matter. All that matters is "Can you make me feel good? Can you affirm me, meet my need, tell me happy stories and make me laugh? If you have that kind of charisma, you'll go right to the top!"

Unfortunately, we Pentecostals seem to care more about style in the pulpit and a flare for the fashionable than we do for character. If the crowds are large, people are healed, and seekers are slain, then there is little concern if the preacher leaves his wife for an intern, supports a lavish lifestyle from offerings, or preaches "feel-good, psychobabble" sermons void of sound doctrine.

But as we've noted, the same charisma that draws a crowd can also propel a man beyond what his character is equipped to sustain. It's a "Charisma Deception." It's when the church places more emphasis on charisma than character and on style more than substance. It's when that misjudgment enables an entire ministry to be built upon a faulty foundation.

What we need is revival. Not a revival of healing or prophesy or supernatural signs. Nor do we need a televised pseudo-revival that fosters hyped-up spiritualism driven by celebrities and techno worship. What we need is a revival of character—a genuine move of God that returns the church to simple values like integrity, humility, and holiness—especially in leaders.

THE CRY OF THE CROWD

Like Saul, good leaders will have many good opportunities to be promoted. There will always be a group of people in search of a new leader who offers them the hope of a better future. The challenge for the leader is to distinguish a "good" opportunity from the "right" opportunity. Just because the crowd is cheering and an offer is appealing, does not mean it is right. In fact, these offers can often be ploys of the devil to move one out of God's will.

In Genesis 13, Lot was offered the opportunity to occupy the lush plains of the Jordan. Sadly, he didn't realize this choice was filled with temptations that would land him to live in bondage among the Sodomites, destroy his family, and ruin his posterity. It was a good opportunity, but not the right opportunity for one so easily tempted.

In Numbers 22, Balaam was offered riches and honor to serve the king of Moab as his personal prophet. It seemed like a good opportunity, but in truth it was a test to reveal what was in his heart. God knew Balaam's heart was filled with lust for the wealth of Moab, He was just using this opportunity to expose it. Perhaps it seemed like a good opportunity, but it was not the right opportunity.

In 2 Samuel 2, Ishbosheth was presented with an opportunity when General Abner offered to position him as king. Unfortunately, Abner was manipulating Ishbosheth to promote himself—a ploy which eventually resulted in the young man's beheading. Again, it seemed like a good opportunity but it was not the right opportunity.

The cry of the crowd and the offer of a good opportunity can never be the deciding factors in a leader's promotion. To follow this course will only bring one to encounter circumstances God never intended and face temptations he or she has not been prepared to face. The result, as we see from Saul, is frustration, pain, and, ultimately, failure.

Every opportunity we face must always be tempered by something deeper in our hearts. It is the desire to always be in the perfect will of God according to His perfect timing. For the true servant of God, this is the only opportunity that is right—and good.

For example, consider David who, because of his good nature and excellent skills, was offered numerous opportunities. Fortunately for David, he never confused what was "good" with what was "right."

In 1 Samuel 16, a young David was anointed the next king of Israel by the prophet Samuel. But, David never mistook Samuel's prophecy as "his opportunity" or as "good timing" for promotion. While others may have been incited by such an affirmation to undermine and depose Saul, David realized the only "right action" for him was to remain humble, return to the hillside tending his sheep and wait for God to promote him.

In 1 Samuel 18, after a winning dramatic victory over Goliath and spurring the army on to battle, David was adored by the crowds. They sang, *"Saul has killed his thousands and David his ten thousands."* Some may have seen that as a good opportunity for promotion, but not David. He knew it would not have been right and instead chose the perfect timing of God over the impulse of man.

In 1 Samuel 22, David was living in the cave of Adullam with four hundred men and their families. Some may consider that a good opportunity to assert their right to lead. But having such a following never emboldened him to divide the nation away from Saul and start his own kingdom.

In 1 Samuel 24, he had a good opportunity to kill Saul and end his plight as a fugitive. With one stroke of a knife, he could have ascended to the throne and began the reign for which he had been anointed. But David discerned that this "good" opportunity was not the "right" opportunity. Instead he spared Saul's life and trusted God to promote him at the right time without having to compromise himself.

Good opportunities are not always right opportunities. Each person must be able to look past the cry of the crowd and hear the leading of God. Missing this can be devastating. For if it is true that the will of God never leads you where the grace of God cannot keep you, then it is also true that moving out of God's will also moves you away from that grace that sustains you. There will be conflicts God never intended you to confront, temptations for which God never planned a way of escape, threats, attacks, and dangers for which you have never been prepared to encounter.

By the same token, remaining in the will of God, even if it means "missing a good opportunity," will always put you in the exact place at the right time for the purpose He has intended. Such has been the case throughout this author's career. There were opportunities in ministry to elevate from the second chair to the first; opportunities to take lucrative careers in the corporate world; opportunities to leave my present church for much larger ones; opportunities for missionary work in exotic countries, and much more. From a professional perspective, many of these opportunities would have brought more promotion, prestige, and more compensation. But good is not always right. By taking an opportunity that appeals to ambition without being Spirit-led, one may actually undermine the plan of God and miss those divine appointments He is arranging for the future.

THE PRIDE OF AMBITION

It could hardly be said that Saul's premature promotion was the result of Saul promoting himself. When the call to lead first came to him, he hid hoping to avoid the appointment (1 Samuel 10:22). At first glance, Saul did not seem to be ruled by ambition or driven by pride.

However, there was something in him that allowed it to happen. Something in him that couldn't refuse, couldn't grieve over the rebellion that brought him the opportunity; there was something in him that said "Yes, I am available. Yes, I'll be your man. I'll take the lead. I'll take the authority that you've refused to God."

It's called ambition. And Saul shows us that regardless of how humble or pure of motive we try to be, the heart is never free from ambition. There will always be a prideful desire to promote one's self to a higher place.

Jeremiah 45:5 warns: *"...do you seek great things for yourself? Do not seek them."* Unfortunately, the Kingdom of God is rampant with ambitious souls whose leadership careers are defined by seeking "great things." Such was the case of Saul. Though initially masked by a display of humility, his ambition was betrayed by his willingness to usurp God's role as Israel's only Monarch.

This is a common scenario in the body of Christ today. It occurs in countless churches throughout the world when a subordinate's ambition pits him or her against the authorities he or she is supposed to submit to. Full of misguided zeal and inflated egos, these usurpers esteem themselves better than their leaders and set out to undermine their authority. They politic and manipulate and maneuver themselves into favorable standing with key people while skillfully inserting seeds of contention against senior leaders.

Absalom was a young man with incredible potential for leadership. However, instead of waiting on God's perfect timing, he set out to promote himself. 2 Samuel 15 records how he shamefully diverted the loyalty of the people away from the king (God's appointed authority) and unto himself. It was a blatant attempt to usurp authority and was swiftly met with God's judgment (2 Samuel 18:14-15).

Lucifer was another leader in the Kingdom of God who subverted authority. Because of certain descriptions of his being that included musical ability connected to worship and leadership, theologians speculate that Lucifer was the worship leader in heaven (Isaiah 14:12-14 and Ezekiel 28:12-15). But instead of directing worship to God, he diverted it from God and unto himself. As a result, the first church of heaven split in two with one third of the angels following their new leader—renamed Satan—into a path of rebellion.

The self-promoting attitude that drove Lucifer's rebellion is the same attitude revealed in our modern day Absaloms: *"I will ascend...I will exalt my...I will also sit on the mount of the congregation"* (Isaiah 14:13). Instead of fostering a spirit of submission and loyalty which are what ultimately qualifies one for greatness in the Kingdom of God, these opportunists grow impatient, divide loyalties unto themselves, and launch a movement that lands them eventually (albeit prematurely) in a position of kingdom authority. The lesson, however, is clear: whenever one acts in subversion against his or her leader, it is an act of demonic rebellion as old as Lucifer himself.

If it happened to King David and if it happened to the King of Glory, it may very well happen to you. There comes a time in many organizations when the people will question or harbor contentions against their leaders. Furthermore, instead of resolving their conflict appropriately, they may look toward subordinate leaders to champion their cause by undermining the senior authority and raising a rebellion against him or her. If—or when—this happens, subordinate leaders must guard themselves against the deceptive voice of pride that whispers: "Your leader is no longer anointed. You should take over. You're anointed. You're loved." Do not fall prey to Absalom's error of believing that such promotion is God's will; you may actually be falling prey to the manipulations of the spirit of Lucifer.

DOES THE DEVIL HAVE AN INTEREST IN YOUR PROMOTION?

If you are eager to be promoted, if you feel that your gifting or ability entitles you to a higher office, I offer this word of caution: The devil may have in interest in your promotion. The enemy may have a foothold on something in your life and he knows that as you are enlarged, his foothold will become a stronghold that he can exploit to ruin the work of God.

Knowing this, the devil may be manipulating circumstances and urging you to canvass for promotion. But don't outrun the perfect timing of God! While it is true that you have great abilities, there may be things in your heart that God is trying to purge. He may be holding you down in humility to cleanse your heart of pride, or exposing areas of impurity to rid your mind of lust. He may be keeping you in want to drive away covetousness. Remember, whatever greatness you are destined for, God must first enlarge your character to support that greatness. Too many, having been promoted prematurely, have been top heavy in their success only to fall and bring destruction on themselves, their families, and the Kingdom of God.

Therefore, I hope you will have the courage to pray the prayer of the humble. Rather than pleading for promotion, our prayer should be: "Lord do not allow me to be promoted beyond what my character will be able to support. Lord, prevent my advancement, shut the door on my ambitions until my heart has been prepared to withstand the temptations, struggles, and pressures that such advancement will certainly bring. Amen."

Then he waited seven days, according to the time set by Samuel. But Samuel did not come to Gilgal; and the people were scattered from him. So Saul said, "Bring a burnt offering and peace offerings here to me." And he offered the burnt offering.

Now it happened, as soon as he had finished presenting the burnt offering, that Samuel came; and Saul went out to meet him, that he might greet him. And Samuel said, "What have you done?" Saul said, "When I saw that the people were scattered from me, and that you did not come within the days appointed, and that the Philistines gathered together at Michmash, then I said, 'The Philistines will now come down on me at Gilgal, and I have not made supplication to the LORD.' Therefore I felt compelled, and offered a burnt offering."

And Samuel said to Saul, "You have done foolishly. You have not kept the commandment of the LORD your God, which He commanded you. For now the LORD would have established your kingdom over Israel forever. But now your kingdom shall not continue. The LORD has sought for Himself a man after His own heart, and the LORD has commanded him to be commander over His people, because you have not kept what the LORD commanded you."

1 Samuel 13:8-14

LESSON TWO

SAUL USURPED HIS LEADER

"Never is integrity more on trial than when one is out of sync with his leader. Loyalty in times of disagreement is the truest test of character."

Gregg Johnson

"You have done foolishly!" was the rebuke of the prophet to the king. Further, the prophet Samuel announced that Saul's kingdom would soon come to an end. Because of his foolish mistake, God revoked the king's authority and would raise another to replace him.

What did he do that was so terrible? What sin had Saul committed that was so heinous in the sight of God that it brought about harsh condemnation and swift rejection? Was it greed or adultery? Was it idolatry or murder? No, but it was something equally destructive for leaders in the Kingdom of God: Saul usurped the authority of his leader.

Following the instructions given to him in 1 Samuel 10:8, the king was to convene a public assembly at Gilgal and wait seven days for his spiritual authority, Samuel the prophet, to arrive. Upon arrival, Samuel would offer sacrifice and receive divine instructions for the king. But Saul disregarded the limits of his civic authority by presenting a burnt offering—a sacred act usually conducted by one bearing spiritual authority. Rather than patiently submitting to Samuel's directive, Saul acted presumptuously, exceeded his initiative and did what he had no right to do.

Never is one's character more on display than when he is out of sync with his leader. It may be a season of patiently waiting; it may be an issue of disagreement; it could even be a matter of disrespect and contempt that one holds toward his authority. It any event, it is how one responds to his authorities in times of disparity that reveals the true quality of his or her character.

"But I'm under God's authority!" This is the foremost objection people raise against submitting toward human authority. Because of their relationship with God or close communion to His presence, they feel that submission to a man is beneath them. However, nothing can be further from the truth.

Anyone can be humble before God; however, true humility is not demonstrated until we humble ourselves before man. Hebrews 13:17 commands: *"Obey those who rule over you, and be submissive, for they watch out for your souls, as those who must give account. Let them do so with joy and not with grief, for that would be unprofitable for you."* Andrew Murray wrote: *"It's easy to think that we are humble before God, but our humility toward others is the proof that our humility before God is real."* In other words, God is not impressed when you humble yourself before Him. Any fool can do that. What impresses God is one's willingness to humble himself before other people. This is especially true when those people seem less powerful, less talented, less intelligent, and less capable

Jesus said, *"Blessed are the meek for they shall inherit the earth."* He said this in contrast to a world that sees meekness as weakness. In the world, meekness provokes images of insecurity and frailty and an inability to stand strong. Whereas, strength is demonstrated by asserting one's will, pushing one's agenda, or "getting my way." But in the Kingdom, strength is actually quite the reverse. In the Kingdom of God, strength is demonstrated by "meekness."

Nowhere is this better demonstrated than in the example of our Lord. Jesus said of Himself, *"I am meek and lowly in heart"* (Matthew 11:29). No one had more power, more ability than Jesus Christ the Son of God, but He humbled Himself and submitted His will to the will of man. Meekness isn't weakness; it is strength under control. Meekness is the awareness that one is strong and talented and capable but chooses not to act on that strength or assert his ability in deference to the will and wishes of another—usually his leader.

"But I hear from God directly!" Many in the Body of Christ today believe God speaks to them directly. Often they call themselves "prophet" or "prophetess," or sometimes they are average laypeople who feel God has given them a specific word on an issue. "God spoke to me!" they say. Or, "I've heard from God on this matter!" Convinced their words are from God, they believe submission to authority does not apply. Even more, they believe authorities should submit to them. It is the usurping of authority in the classic sense. I've seen where "prophets" intimidate pastors and manipulate and control churches all under the guise of "I've heard from God directly, therefore you must obey me."

Let's be clear. There is only one source of authoritative word from God: The Bible! 2 Timothy 3:16 says, *"All Scripture is given by inspiration of God, and is profitable for doctrine, for reproof, for correction, for instruction in righteousness."* All other "Words from God" are subject to the evaluation of God's written Word and the approval of appropriate authorities.

While it is true that some may prophesy today, these "prophets" do not operate under the same mandate as did prophets in the Old Testament. In the Old Testament, God spoke directly to the prophet; the message was authoritative because the spirit of the prophet was subject to the leading of the Holy Spirit (2 Peter 1:21). But today, God speaks by the "inner witness" of the Spirit (Romans 8:16, John 16:13). The message is not absolute (e.g. Jeremiah) but is filtered through the impressions and opinions of our inner man. 1 Corinthians 14:32 implies this by stating *"...the spirits of the prophets are subject to the prophets."* Indeed, the prophetic word may be from God, but it is also from you, and has been filtered through your flesh, your feelings, and your subjective opinions. It is tainted by your humanity and is not a pure word from God.

This is why 1 Corinthians 14:29 reads: *"Let two or three prophets speak, and let the others judge."* Prophetic words are not absolute and are subject to the evaluation and approval of others who have proper authority. When Old Testament prophets spoke, people simply accepted their words and obeyed (2 Chronicles 20:20). But today, in the church, all believers have God's Spirit and therefore all have the ability to discern the voice and call of God. 1 John 4:1 says, *"Beloved, do not believe every spirit, but test the spirits, whether they are of God; because many false prophets have gone out into the world."* The scriptures are unmistakably clear: WE SHOULD NOT automatically accept prophetic words, but TEST THE SPIRITS FIRST. While it may be true that God is giving a word to a prophet, it is equally true that the prophet's "word" must be qualified as actually being from God.

On this point, 1 Corinthians 14:29 is dogmatic. Just because one may feel an inspiration or an "anointing" to prophesy, that does not give you license to usurp the pastor or spiritual leader and exceed your initiative. The prophet's word must be submitted to others who have the Holy Spirit to confirm it. Give your word to the leader, welcome that leader's evaluation and submit yourself to the leader's judgment. Anything more is an expression of spiritual pride and human ego wanting to be affirmed.

"But how can I submit when the authority over me is wrong?" Anyone can submit when he or she is in agreement with their leader. Saul could have easily obeyed Samuel had Samuel been doing what he was supposed to be doing; it was Samuel's absence and perceived dereliction of duty that tested the sincerity of Saul's submission.

True submission is demonstrated, not in times of agreement, but in seasons of disagreement. In fact, there is no expression of submission without the context of disagreement. Without disagreement, submission is merely compliance. There is no need to restrain one's impulse or force one's obedience; one needs only to agree with that which he already views favorable.

On the contrary, it is one's ability to resist that surge of disagreement rising in one's heart—it is that discipline to quell an impulse of assertiveness against the leader that proves true submission and the presence of real humility.

Consider David before he became king. No one was more

wrong than King Saul and no one was more right than David (1 Samuel 18). In fact, Saul was spiteful, bitter and influenced by evil spirits. David, on the other hand, was singing psalms and killing Philistines. But David never lifted his hand against his authority. The one time David did act against him, he felt great remorse and publicly repented (1 Samuel 24:6). In those times when the authority is wrong, God is not looking for your help. He is more than able to work all things according to His will. More often, God is trying to work out issues of character in His future leaders—issues such as submission, humility, and faithfulness. Sometimes He does that by putting you under a Saul.

"But I have more anointing than the leader!" Not only was David more "right" than Saul, David had more anointing than Saul. In 1 Samuel 16, the prophet Samuel came to David's house and anointed him to be the next king of Israel. But did David march into the throne room and demand Saul to abdicate? Did he start up a new kingdom and draw converts to himself? No, David remained on that hillside, humbly serving those few sheep in obscurity. He didn't exercise initiative, he waited; he patiently deferred to the will and timing of God and let Him do the promoting.

There are only two stations in the Kingdom of God. Either you are under authority or you are in rebellion. Either you are of the spirit of Christ that says "not my will be done" or you are of the spirit of Lucifer that says, *"I will ascend, I will establish my throne, I will exalt myself"* (Isaiah 14:13).

There are far too many "break-away" churches today— congregations that are birthed out of sedition. Too often some brother in a church or visiting minister feels called to lead or believes he has more anointing than the pastor and rallies a group of church members away to start a new church. Rather than submitting to and supporting the leader, these usurpers operate in the spirit of Lucifer who also lusted after authority and caused a split in the First Church of Heaven.

Usually these break-away churches are led by those who establish themselves as prophets, apostles, bishops, and pastors. But they fail to understand that in the Kingdom of God authority can only be given, it is never assumed! It does not matter what your gift, anointing, calling, or ministry is—you cannot confer authority upon yourself. Whoever you are or whatever gifting you have, authority must be given to you by another authority that you remain submitted under and accountable to.

Paul warned against *"...false apostles, deceitful workers, who 'transform themselves' into apostles of Christ"* (2 Corinthians 11:13). These were opportunists who sought to be regarded as spiritual authorities (2 Corinthians 11:12) but operated in an independent spirit. They were not sanctioned by the apostles but had "ordained" themselves. The application for us is clear: self-proclaimed prophets are false prophets, self-proclaimed apostles are false apostles, self-proclaimed pastors are false pastors.

Even Jesus validated His office by the testimony of the authorities that endorsed Him. He said, *"If I bear witness of Myself, My witness is not true"* (John 5:31). He went on to list the authorities that ordained and sanctioned His ministry. If Jesus needed to be ordained through institutions recognizable to man, how much more do we need authority delegated to us by reputable spiritual authorities?

If you're a usurper, beware. Galatians 6:7 warns us: *"Be not deceived; God is not mocked: for whatsoever a man sows, that shall he also reap."* If you birth a church in rebellion, rebellion will be part of your DNA. It's just a matter of time until you become a victim of rebellion and some usurpers rise up to break away from you.

KNOW THE LIMITS OF YOUR AUTHORITY

Sadly, King Saul shows us a mistake that is common to many. At certain times and under certain conditions, some will believe themselves to be exempt from submission. Samuel delayed. He was late. Samuel failed to fulfill his responsibility—at least that was what Saul thought. So Saul felt entitled to take initiative, usurp the command of his spiritual leader, act on his own initiative and even undermine his authority—all under the guise of "it's what's right for the people."

Ultimately, this isn't about "what's right for the people." It's really about submission and Saul's unwillingness to submit. Saul didn't think submission applied to him. He was the king, the expert, the anointed one. He was supposed to have all the answers—why should he submit and wait?

Essentially, Saul had forgotten his place. He had been promoted to a position of authority but lost sight of the limits of that authority, overstepped his boundaries and took on a responsibility that wasn't his to assume. Those who've received the privilege to serve as leaders, must remember what Saul forgot. Deacons and ministry staff beware. Elders, trustees and board members take heed. There is a limit to your authority, a boundary to how far you can lead, and a line that, if not careful, you can cross.

King Uzziah crossed that line. 2 Chronicles 26:16-21 describes his great success, how he prospered the nation and established Judah as a military superpower. However, when he became strong *"...his heart was lifted up."* Like Saul, Uzziah believed himself superior to those around him—even the priests. He reasoned: "I am king. God has favored me above all other men. Thousands of souls bow before me. Why must I defer to some cleric to offer incense for me? I can burn my own incense—I have a 'special' relationship with God and need not submit to a lowly priest."

With this attitude, Uzziah entered the sanctuary and offered incense to God—a blatant violation of mosaic protocol. Immediately, the high priest along with eighty others confronted the king and said, *"It is not for you, Uzziah, to burn incense to the Lord, but for the priests, the sons of Aaron, who are consecrated to burn incense. Get out of the sanctuary, for you have trespassed! You shall have no honor from the Lord God."* As a result, God judged Uzziah by striking him with leprosy—a sign of spiritual uncleanness and public humiliation. King Uzziah, because he was presumptuous and usurped authority, remained leprous until the day of his death.

THE PERIL OF PRESUMPTION

Presumption is the stench of a prideful heart—and God hates the smell of pride. King Uzziah shows us it can occur after one ascends to a position of authority or achieves some level of success. Having felt that surge of confidence that comes from achievement, the leader begins to feel important. His ego inflates. He becomes over confident. His heart, now filled with pride, tells him, "Because I have a title, because I have authority and a position, I have certain rights and privileges that allow me to speak or act or initiate as I see fit." And so these leaders, emboldened by this "self awareness," forget their place and usurp the structures of authority and protocol around them.

It is presumption; it is pride, and it is offensive to God. Superficially, the incense that Uzziah offered was that same sweet smelling incense usually offered by the priests. It had the same pleasing flavor, the same attractive color and aroma. To the untrained eye, it had every appearance of being holy and genuine. But what seemed to be legitimate was actually a stench in the nostrils of God. It was polluted incense that flowed from a presumptuous, self-promoting heart; it was the stench of pride.

The lesson is clear: we must be very careful about assuming such rights and privileges for ourselves—regardless of how "spiritual" or "gifted" we seem to be. Some well-meaning souls, although hoping to "do good for God," have actually offered the incense of Uzziah.

"SO HOW DO I ADDRESS DISAGREEMENTS WITH MY LEADERS?"

Concern for spiritual presumption is not to say that Christians should never disagree with or challenge the authorities over them. Spiritual leaders are not authoritarian demigods wielding absolute power in the name of Christ; they are mere people—infallible flesh that often makes mistakes and exercises severe lapses in judgment. As such, there are times when leaders should be challenged. The question is "how" such authorities can be challenged without compromising our own humility and sense of integrity.

If you have a concern, there are ways to address it righteously. The first way is through intercessory warfare. Pray! God may have burdened your spirit with an issue or given you insight on a matter—not so you can call everyone on the phone and tell them what the authority is doing wrong—but so you can pray with fervor, wisdom, and divine unction. Ezekiel 22:31 says that God is seeking for men and women to stand in the gap. He is looking for intercessors to pray. The way He finds them is by burdening them with revelation and seeing who will be faithful to call down His will. It is my conviction that no one has a right to speak on a matter, criticize a leader, or canvass for change until they have first spent ample time covering the matter in prayer, interceding for His will, and checking their own attitude.

Secondly, submit your concern to your spiritual authority with a right spirit. If you must, go to your pastor—but go with a humble, submissive attitude. Instead of being forceful, be teachable. Ask him to help you understand why "such and such" is being permitted or if he has considered another perspective. Many times, a pastor will reject a suggestion out of hand because of the spirit in which it was presented. Conversely, if you present an idea with meekness, he will be more inclined to accept it because it has a quality of godliness and goodwill upon it.

Thirdly, refrain from using the phrase "God told me to tell you" or "God showed me." Clearly, scripture does show that God speaks to people today, and you may sincerely believe He is speaking to you. But, the wise communicator understands such statements can seem manipulative. In other words, some so-called "prophets" assert divine authority to compel others into agreement. They are removing any option for disagreement—and if one does disagree, the prophet can salvage his self-respect by labeling that one as ignorant and unspiritual. If your word really is from God, let the wisdom and power of the word speak for itself. Why should anyone need to be convinced of its authenticity or intimidated into accepting it as "a word from God?" Instead, follow the words of James 3:17 that says, *"the wisdom from above is peaceable, gentle and easy to be entreated."*

A FINAL WORD

Clearly, God considers spiritual presumption so egregious that it will disqualify one called to lead. In fact, it is such an offense to God that He subjects leaders to conditions that expose any trace of it. It is this author's belief that Samuel purposely waited to the last day of the seven in order to test Saul's character—to determine if he was truly fit for the high office God called him to. Of course, he was not and God rejected him.

Ambitious and aspiring leaders must take heed from the examples of Saul and Uzziah. Indeed you may sincerely want to correct a wrong. Perhaps you truly have heard from God and want to assert your revelation. Maybe you are wiser and better equipped than those who are authorities over you. But beware, the situation before you may not be as obvious as you think. It may seem like Samuel is late and it's up to you to offer a sacrifice; but it could actually be a test designed by God to purge you of spiritual presumption and reveal if you are qualified for greater promotion.

How The Mighty Have Fallen

And the men of Israel were distressed that day, for Saul had placed the people under oath, saying, "Cursed is the man who eats any food until evening, before I have taken vengeance on my enemies." So none of the people tasted food. Now all the people of the land came to a forest; and there was honey on the ground. And when the people had come into the woods, there was the honey, dripping; but no one put his hand to his mouth, for the people feared the oath. But Jonathan had not heard his father charge the people with the oath; therefore he stretched out the end of the rod that was in his hand and dipped it in a honeycomb, and put his hand to his mouth; and his countenance brightened. Then one of the people said, "Your father strictly charged the people with an oath, saying, 'Cursed is the man who eats food this day.'" And the people were faint. But Jonathan said, "My father has troubled the land. Look now, how my countenance has brightened because I tasted a little of this honey. How much better if the people had eaten freely today of the spoil of their enemies which they found! For now would there not have been a much greater slaughter among the Philistines?"

1 Samuel 14:24-30

LESSON THREE

SAUL ABUSED HIS AUTHORITY

"Those who have been once intoxicated with power, and have derived any kind of emolument from it, never can willingly abandon it."

Edmund Burke

Saul was obsessed with establishing his greatness. But the price of his ambition was the abuse of the people he was called to serve. He wanted a dynasty, an empire that would stand for ages to come. He wanted a name that all the earth would adore and revere. But to do this, he exploited his people. He forbade them from eating, resting, or tending to their own needs until his victory was sure. In fact, he pronounced a curse upon any who refused to cooperate. It mattered not how distressed, fatigued, or hungry they were. All that mattered was his ambition. Driven by a perverted vision of greatness, Saul believed that Israel existed to serve him rather than him for it. Instead of esteeming the people as a trust God had given him to shepherd and protect, he saw them as things to use to fulfill his own lust for success.

Sadly, the same self-serving spirit that drove King Saul is a force growing more common in the body of Christ: Christian leaders using their office, not to glorify God or edify His people, but to promote themselves. At first glance it appears their cause is noble. They seem to be serving people and advancing the Kingdom of God; but closer examination reveals something different. There is a subtle tendency to manipulate others, to control and use them like objects to advance the leader's ambition.

LEADERSHIP IS A TRUST

Authority is God's idea. It is God's way of providing a fair and equitable means of maintaining order and stability throughout His creation. It is the right to govern, exercise leadership, initiate an action, or give commands. It flows from a position granted to an individual by a higher authority or by the consent of the governed. In this sense, leadership is a trust given to the leader to serve the needs of the people, not his own. People are submitting to him because they trust he will have their best interests and the interests of the organization as his motive. This means that a leader's actions and decisions should never be designed for his own personal benefits or to advance his interests.

Unfortunately, as with anything God bestows to humanity, authority is often perverted and abused by the wickedness of man's heart. Eighteenth-century philosopher Edmund Burke wrote, *"Those who have been once intoxicated with power, and have derived any kind of emolument from it, never can willingly abandon it."* In other words, authority is like a drug that intoxicates a leader with an illicit sense of power. Having tasted that power, the leader becomes addicted to it and abuses it. Lord Acton said it like this: *"Power corrupts and absolute power corrupts absolutely."*

CORRUPTION OF LEADERSHIP

Corruption is the abuse of public office or position for private gain. It is when something good turns bad. It is when good leaders, who begin with noble intentions, become enticed and corrupted by selfish opportunities. They cease to use their authority to serve the public good and, instead, use their position to better themselves, solicit favors, amass wealth, promote friends and family, and leverage power to themselves. This is what happened to Saul. He used his authority as a means to achieve his own ambitions.

Corruption, however, is not restricted to kings and politicians. It can be seen wherever people have power over other people, even in the church.

In East and West Africa, there has been massive growth in Pentecostal churches. Unfortunately, much of the resurgence is driven by preachers taking advantage of poor, illiterate people by asking them for financial contributions in the belief that in return, they would be blessed with wealth. Many of these "spiritual authorities" rarely have any formal religious training and are known to resort to tricks, gimmicks, and outright deception to demonstrate their "special anointing" and touch from God.

Recently, a Ghanaian pastor arrived at Entebbe Airport in Uganda only to find police waiting for him. Local law enforcement had been informed that a Pentecostal pastor was trying to bring a device that delivers an electric shock into the country. A search of his luggage revealed a magician's instrument called the "Electric Touch Machine." It consisted of a battery pack, some wires, and electrodes. The device amplifies static electricity on your body and enables you to deliver an electric shock to whatever (or whomever) you touch. The pastor, allegedly, would use it during altar calls. Supposedly, people would come for prayer and, by laying hands on them, he would impart an enhanced static shock, leading them to believe they received an electrified anointing from the Holy Spirit.[1]

In London, England, a famous Kenyan pastor was arrested for trafficking babies out of Nairobi. He claimed to have an anointed touch that enabled infertile women to become pregnant. The "miracle" involved the pastor performing an exorcism on the infertile woman which supposedly cleanses her soul, followed by his declaration that she is now pregnant. After only a couple weeks of pregnancy the minister takes women to Nairobi to "give birth" in the slum clinics. However, DNA tests have proven that 21 of these "miracle babies" have no biological link to their supposed parents and further medical evidence proved the women were not pregnant before the "births." Apparently babies were taken from slum families and given to these women for whom they would pay a handsome fee.[2]

In Nigeria, broadcasters are no longer allowed to show miracles on television in a way which is not "provable and believable." Nigeria's National Broadcasting Commission says television stations that fail to abide by the ruling will be fined, and their equipment could be confiscated. This comes in response to recurrent Nigerian TV broadcasts featuring Pentecostal services that center on alleged miracles. Many of their preachers claim to cure diseases or bring wealth and happiness but never substantiate their claims. The result is many poor and uneducated people flock to these services only to be taken advantage of by Pentecostal conmen.[3]

In Uganda, corruption among Pentecostal leaders has become such an epidemic that Uganda's office of Ethics and Integrity has taken interest. "We feel there is a need for a policy on religion," the director told the BBC's *Network Africa* program. Denying that the government was interfering in people's private lives, he said, "When matters go to impinging on the stability of the country, I think the government gets interested."[4]

In this groundswell of spiritual exploitation, church leaders must recognize that the cancer of corruption has infected even the Pentecost and Charismatic movement. When spiritual leaders, entrusted with sacred duties, leverage their authority to manipulate people and misappropriate resources for personal, private gain, it is corrupt. Whether it is a promise to facilitate anointing, provide a blessing, or work a miracle, the leader is positioned to benefit personally from the suffering or sacrifice of the one he is supposed to serve.

SPIRITUAL EXTORTION

They preach to the crowds with hypnotic charisma as the people hang on every word. They call themselves prophets and cry, "Sow your money into this ministry today, and you will reap of harvest of blessing. Miss this opportunity and you may never receive the miracle you need." When the baskets are passed, people give generously. They are convinced that their giving will move God to bless them. Even worse, to not give would cause God's hand to withdraw.

The legal world defines extortion as obtaining money or goods from another through intimidation, manipulation or threats. While no one is threatening bodily harm or holding a gun to anyone's head—the words spoken by the "man of God" have the same effect. People are intimidated through fear, manipulated by emotion and threatened by "the Word of God" to give their money right now or suffer the consequences. It may not be considered extortion in a court of law—but it is in the spirit. What looks like a normal church offering—is a shameful attempt to extort money from the people of God. Like Saul, they use and exploit the people to enlarge the scope of their "ministry kingdom."

I was utterly amazed when one internationally-renowned evangelist told his television audience, "How can you expect to make the rapture when you are keeping 'God's money' in your bank account?" Now, I believe in tithing, and I agree that believers should give offerings, but this was a blatant attempt to force money out of people through fear. Another famous "prophetess" told her viewers that if you want God to protect your loved ones, you need to declare Psalm 91 over their life and give $91.00 as an expression of your faith ($910.00 might even bring a greater miracle).

If extortion is to coerce money through intimidation, manipulation or threats—then this is it! Spiritual extortion is using faith, authority and God's Word to scare people into giving. When vulnerable and needy people are told by trusted leaders that relief from their suffering is conditional upon giving money in the offering, then they are no better than mobsters extorting money with the promise of *"protection."*

As leaders, we should always be motivated by love. People are not things we use to promote ourselves by providing what we need to achieve our ambitions. They aren't "checkbooks" and "Visa cards" meant to finance our ambitions. That is corrupt! They are the "Church—the Body of Christ." They are the precious saints God has called us to serve and train in the principles of His Word.

MAINTAINING TRUST AS A LEADER

There is no greater protection a leader has against corruption than the heart of a servant. This is one reason why Jesus made it a prerequisite for leaders in the Kingdom of God. He knew that in a very short time, after His ascension and the outpouring of the Holy Spirit, thousands would be saved and the disciples would be given charge over large sums of money. Acts 4 tells how *"... all who were possessors of lands or houses sold them, and brought the proceeds of the things that were sold, and laid them at the apostles' feet; and they distributed to each as anyone had need"* (Acts 4:34-35). Clearly, because the apostles saw themselves as servants of the people, they were able to distribute these assets without acting like Judas who was a *"'thief'...and used to take what was put in the money bag for his own use"* (John 12:6).

In order to maintain trust as a leader, there are certain basic principles that must be in place. Both followers and outsiders alike must be able to look closely at the leader and clearly discern that he or she is using his or her authority for the good of the people and not for himself or herself.

TRUST IS MAINTAINED
THROUGH ACCOUNTABILITY

Accountability implies answerability. It occurs when one

party is obliged to report to another party regarding his actions and decisions in order to justify them or to suffer punishment in the case of misconduct. In essence, it means that no one leader or group of leaders is autonomous, but is surrounded by a system of checks and balances that places boundaries on his authority.

Pride thrives and corruption occurs where there is a vacuum of accountability. Whenever a leader is free to act without fear of reprisal, he will usually act selfishly; to believe anything less is naive. King David was Israel's greatest leader; he was a man after God's own heart. However, at the moment David felt free of accountability, he used his power selfishly. He exercised his influence over kingdom personnel to have Bathsheba brought to himself and raped her. He then used his authority over the military to have her husband moved to the frontlines and killed in battle.

When a leader has no accountability, he will abuse his authority. It is a sad fact of human leadership that has no exceptions. The words of Lord Acton reinforce this truth: "Power corrupts and absolute power corrupts absolutely."

TRUST IS MAINTAINED
THROUGH ACTS OF SERVICE

The more a leader succeeds, the harder it is for him to maintain a servant's heart. It's easy to be humble when one is just starting out. He is willing to take on any task, or do any job without complaint. But after he becomes successful and gains titles, he becomes less inclined to do menial or unpleasant tasks. "Those tasks," he starts to believe, "are for other less important, less notable people." Getting a drink for someone, sweeping a dirty floor, cleaning a bathroom, opening a door for a stranger, or greeting a child, can seem as being below his stature. But these acts of service are exactly what leaders need to maintain their humility and trust as a leader.

At the heart of corruption is the leader's belief that he or she is more important than the people he or she leads. This is especially true in the church. Many, believing themselves to have some unique anointing or special calling, confer upon themselves the titles of apostle, prophet, or doctor and adorn themselves with certificates and honorary degrees. Others claim to have an extraordinary relationship with God that gives them the right to dominate and control followers. Others highlight their authority by asserting deep spiritual experiences and spirit-induced revelations. A few leaders will even twist Scripture out of context and re-interpret traditional doctrine to suit their own special revelations. Other prideful leaders teach that God operates through a hierarchy or "chain of command" and the leader, of course, is the key link in that chain acting as God's prophet or mediator between the follower and God.

However, no matter how "anointed" or elevated a leader becomes, he is never greater than when performing menial acts of service for those in need. The greatest example of this is Jesus stooping down to wash the filthy feet of His disciples. He could have reminded them that He was Almighty God and they should wash His feet, but He didn't; instead, He poured the water over their dirt stained feet and scrubbed and rinsed and dried them by His own hand. In the same way, the leader who is willing to sweep a floor, clean a bathroom, visit the elderly, or personally touch those in need, will never lose sight of his true calling—to serve those he is called to lead.

Conducting acts of service has a way of keeping our feet on the ground—the same ground that Jesus walked. We must never forget that He who is King of kings and Lord of lords made Himself of no reputation, took the form of a bondservant and came in the likeness of men. He humbled Himself and became obedient to the point of death, even the death of the cross (Philippians 2:7-8).

TRUST IS MAINTAINED THROUGH TRANSPARENCY

In leadership structures, transparency is a means of examining the practices and policies of public officials and preventing corruption. It is when a government's decision-making processes are open to the public and the press. Transparency or "open government" allows budgets and financial statements to be reviewed by anyone while at the same time the leader's decisions, rules, laws, and policies are open to discussion or criticism. Such practices of openness prevent the opportunity for authorities to abuse the system for their own interests.

Whenever leaders close their administration to public scrutiny or supervision, they are inviting corruption and undermining their trust. Just as mold and rust grow in dark, unventilated areas, leadership becomes corrupt where there is no transparency to expose inequity or openness to aerate greed. Oversight and openness are the light and ventilation of leadership protecting it from corruption.

Unfortunately, many church leaders today are threatened by transparency. Like dictators guarding their power, they see authority as something to be ardently defended. Any attempt to question or scrutinize one's decision is viewed as a threat to be retarded. Financial matters are treated as top secret decisions and people who inquire regarding procedures are seen as enemies vying for power. The result is organizations that lack credibility and integrity because they have become the private fiefdoms of the leaders who control them.

TRUST IS MAINTAINED THROUGH COLLABORATION

Collaboration is working in concert with others to promote creativity, synergy, and mutual accountability. It's surrounding yourself with the right people and being able to work with them without trying to control them. In fact, successful leaders understand that the people you surround yourself with will determine how high you can go—or how quickly you may fail.

Scripture shows us that collaborative leaders are trusted leaders whom God can promote. Proverbs 11:14 says: *"Where there is no counsel, the people fall; but in the multitude of counselors there is safety."* More to the point, when God is getting ready to promote or enlarge a leader, one of the first things He does is surround that leader with good people. Moses had Aaron, Hur, Jethro and Joshua. David had his mighty men and Sons of Issachar who understood the times. Hezekiah had Isaiah, Esther had Mordecai, and even Jesus had Peter, James, and John. And when Paul was first saved, God gave him a special encourager named Barnabus.

But these "encouragers" are not there to simply agree with and affirm the leader. They're also there as a system of checks and balances. Every leader needs checks and balances. This is especially true the larger the leader's scope of authority and the amount of people he influences.

Collaborative supporters of the leader (e.g., deacons, elders, trustees, subordinate staff) are like eyeglasses perfecting the leader's vision. Every leader has vision, but sees through a glass darkly—his vision is never a perfect 20/20. This is why the leader needs a Jethro or an Isaiah or a Barnabus. They act like eyeglasses placed over our imperfect vision to add clarity, focus, and refinement. They take the blur out of our vision and help us to aim the organization more accurately.

However, this benefit can only be realized when the leader is collaborative.[5] Jim Collins explains that the worst kind of leaders are the autocratic, type-A, charismatic, power-driven personalities. Ironically, these are the leaders the world seems to admire. However. they actually undermine the collaborative dynamic in most organizations. These kinds of leaders are what Collins calls "the genius with a thousand helpers." They are not open to ideas and hinder collaboration by their strong personalities. They demand agreement and submission and have little tolerance for dissenting opinions. Although this kind of leadership may work well on a military battlefield, it has little success in corporate, civic, and not-for-profit organizations.

Collins goes on to reveal the "Good to Great" leaders who led their companies to extreme success were democratic and collaborative. The strategy for their success laid in the group's dialogue and shared insights of a talented executive team. It was the leader who saw himself, not as a dictator, but as a servant of the team that promoted such free exchange of ideas and healthy discussion. As well, their style of mutual respect and peer accountability promoted both confidence and loyalty in the teams they led. In short, their teams "trusted" and felt safe around them.

TRUST IS MAINTAINED THROUGH HEALTHY RELATIONSHIPS

The more I serve in leadership, the more I realize that the most important things are not vision statements, strategic planning or budget projections; the most important things are relationships. The health of any organization rises or falls on the health of the relationships that make up that organization—more specifically, the relationships within the leadership team.

Leadership is not simply "getting stuff done," it's getting stuff done through people. It means being able to work with people, motivate them, empower them, and relate to them in a healthy and productive way. The servant leader who has been entrusted with leadership understands this dynamic and dedicates himself to promoting a unified leadership team.

John Maxwell said, *"People don't care how much you know until they know how much your care."* This is equally true among those who comprise the leadership team. Our co-leaders need to know that we care about them and desire their friendship. They need for us to set the tone for trust, mutual respect, camaraderie, and unity.

The prideful, self-centered leader often recoils against this truth. These leaders, because they have an over-inflated sense of themselves, think others should automatically respect them, trust them, and follow them. They resent the fact that they actually have to take the time to invest in others personally and humble themselves to serve them. The leader who fails to grasp the importance of relationships is a failure waiting to happen.

THE TRUST

Leadership is a trust given to us by those we lead. Never should it be used for one's own benefit or personal advancement. That would be an abuse of one's authority. Every decision, action, and reaction should be meant for the advancement and betterment of those we serve and the organization we represent.

If one aspires to leadership out of a desire for power, recognition, or control, he or she is aspiring for the wrong reason. Our ministry will be polluted with impure motives and defiled by worldly ambition. What's worse is it will be void of God's blessing and will actually draw down His curse. James 4:6 says, *"God resists the proud."* Proverbs 16:18 tell us that *"Pride goes before destruction, and a haughty spirit before a fall."* Self promotion provokes God to move against us and pull our ministry down. Humility, on the other hand, invokes God's blessing and rich provision.

How The Mighty Have Fallen

Now go and attack Amalek, and utterly destroy all that they have, and do not spare them. But kill both man and woman, infant and nursing child, ox and sheep, camel and donkey.
1 Samuel 15:3

Now the LORD sent you on a mission, and said, "Go, and utterly destroy the sinners, the Amalekites, and fight against them until they are consumed. Why then did you not obey the voice of the LORD? Why did you swoop down on the spoil, and do evil in the sight of the LORD?" And Saul said to Samuel, "But I have obeyed the voice of the LORD, and gone on the mission on which the LORD sent me, and brought back Agag king of Amalek; I have utterly destroyed the Amalekites. But the people took of the plunder, sheep and oxen, the best of the things which should have been utterly destroyed, to sacrifice to the LORD your God in Gilgal."
1 Samuel 15:18-21

Then Saul said to Samuel, "I have sinned, for I have transgressed the commandment of the LORD and your words, because I feared the people and obeyed their voice."
1 Samuel 15:24

LESSON FOUR

SAUL LOVED MAN'S PRAISE MORE THAN GOD'S APPROVAL

> *"The essence of leadership is to confront status quo and pull the people to the place they ought to be."*
>
> Gregg Johnson

He was the most revered and powerful man in Israel. An entire army obeyed his command. No one compared in status, wealth, and respectability. Yet, by his own admission, Saul "feared the people." As a result of this condition, God deemed the king unfit for leadership and prophesied the removal of his authority. The lesson is clear: in the Kingdom of God it is impossible to lead people when you are afraid of them.

God gave King Saul a clear vision of His will. The Amalekites were to be utterly destroyed as retribution for their mistreatment of Israel years before. Man and beast, woman and child, none were to survive.

Apparently, en route to battle, someone had an idea: "Let's save the plunder, sheep and oxen, and offer them as a sacrifice to God in Gilgal. And while we're at it, let's spare King Agag; he seems like a nice enough fellow and could be a good friend to us." The idea had wide appeal and general consensus determined that destroying "everything" was unnecessary. The result was a new vision—one more suited to the preferences of the people.

The essence of leadership is to confront status quo and pull the people to "the place they ought to be." It often requires the leader to challenge unhealthy cultural norms in the face of disagreement and strong resistance. Although he may be misunderstood, maligned, and even mistreated, it is in those times the leader simply must lead!

This is why God requires leaders to have a unique disposition. He told Jeremiah, *"Do not be afraid of their words or dismayed by their looks...lest I dismay you before them"* (Jeremiah 1:17). He wanted Jeremiah to have a "face like flint"—a sense of hardened determination. This is not a mandate to disregard people's opinions or resist accountability; rather, it is an appeal for leaders to focus on their God-given vision, move relentlessly toward it, and pull the people there by the force of their conviction.

This is exactly what Saul could not do and what disqualified him from leadership. He feared the people, consented to their rebellion, and permitted Agag to live. Samuel would soon teach him that to condone wrong behavior, even tacitly, is to bear as much blame as those who commit the evil blatantly.

THE NATURE OF LEADERSHIP

There is a spirit attacking leaders in the church today. Simply stated, it is a spirit that causes leaders "not to lead."

The nature of leadership is to stand out in front and call others to a higher place, but this spirit causes leaders to lag behind with apathy and malaise. When they should be pointing the way, challenging the prevailing attitudes of mediocrity, this spirit induces leaders to sit idly on the sidelines with hands in pocket blending into the background of status quo.

Where are the leaders? Where are the ones who discern what is evil and recognize what is good—and act upon it! Where are the leaders who refuse to mimic culture and, instead, stand apart from it, and call their people to a higher level? Where are leaders who are more concerned about being righteous than being popular and care more about integrity than being a success?

Where are they? They have gone the way of Saul—mere figureheads having titles of authority but little spiritual authority. They have positions of influence but little power to actually command change in the hearts of their followers. They spare the sheep, let Agag live, and permit the people to feel good about having a pretentious faith that lacks genuine submission to the will of God.

Leadership is not just having a title. It's more than sitting on a committee. Leadership is about movement and change and influencing people toward a certain direction. To lead is to be in the "place" God wants for His people and then "pull" people into that place by the power of one's own passion. It is having such an effect on people that they take ownership of the same attitudes, values, and convictions of the one leading them. Sadly, many believe that because they have a respected title or attend meetings that they function as a leader. They are mistaken. Pastors who fill churches but fail to produce cross-carrying disciples are not leading. Trustees who manage a place of worship but do not show people how to worship in that place are not leading. Deacons who affirm their belief in prayer but do not attend prayer meetings are not leading. Elders who "amen" their agreement with the concept of holiness but do not openly demonstrate repentance and display a passion for personal purity are not leading.

Leaders are "first." They do not wait for an invitation or rely on encouragement from their peers. They lead. Leaders are the first ones to sacrifice, the first ones to give, the first to pray, worship, repent, and weep over sin. They are the first to serve, the first to shout "amen" and the first to the altar for deeper consecration. Leaders constantly look behind at the ranks that follow and challenge complacency by the force of their own example. They do not wait for someone else to determine the environment. They decide how the environment should be and set out to change it. Culture is every leader's battlefield, status quo is the enemy and victory is decided by the transformational results of their influence.

True leadership can be likened to a thermostat regulating the temperature of a room. If the spiritual climate of a house grows cold, the leader turns up the heat by the intensity of his own passion and converts the environment to his own character. On the other hand, leaders having gone the way of Saul are more like thermometers. Instead of influencing the environment, they are influenced by it and conform to it. When watching the character of a Saul, one will not see a passionate example of where God is calling His body to; instead, one will see a mere reflection of the tired lukewarmness that has gripped the community and is destroying it.

LEADERS ARE TRANSFORMATIONAL

Leadership isn't hard when everyone is walking in the same direction. It's only hard when you try to get people to change course.

Some leaders make the mistake of thinking they are leading when all they're doing is tantamount to driving in traffic. Just because all the cars around you are moving in the same direction doesn't mean you are leading them. By the same token, just because you have a crowd around you does not mean you are their leader. Saul had a crowd but he wasn't leading them—he was appeasing them in order to keep them. He wasn't interested in moving people toward the will of God, he wanted a following. Sure, he had a title, a position. But he was no more their leader than was the horse he was riding on.

True leadership has the power to make people change direction. It is transformational. Unfortunately, many of today's "leaders" are no different than Saul. It's not about transforming the character of the crowd, it's about getting and keeping the crowd; it's mostly about numbers. Gather an audience, keep the audience, entertain the audience and you win! Unfortunately, those we often call leaders are nothing more than crowd pleasers, no more valuable to the Kingdom of God than clowns entertaining an audience.

LEADERS UPHOLD GOD'S WORD

The Apostle Paul told his young protégé, *"Preach the word! Be ready in season and out of season. Convince, rebuke, exhort, with all longsuffering and teaching. For the time will come when they will not endure sound doctrine, but according to their own desires, because they have itching ears, they will heap up for themselves teachers; and they will turn their ears away from the truth, and be turned aside to fables"* (2 Timothy 4:2-4).

Something is happening to gospel preaching today. It is losing its power to convince, rebuke, and exhort. Indeed, the crowds are coming in and churches continue to "grow," but is it because the preacher is transformational like Paul, or is it because the leader is itching ears like Saul? One pastor told me, "My church is growing because the people hunger for truth and the gospel has a magnetic draw." I agree, but people also have itching ears and the false gospel gratifies and attracts the flesh. We must be careful not to feel validated because people are drawn to our "magnetic gospel." The question is, are we preaching the whole counsel of God or just those parts that appease the crowd?

It's an important question because too much preaching today avoids the difficult truths of the Word. We don't talk about sin. We don't talk about guilt, wrath and judgment, we certainly don't talk about Hell, and topics such as holiness, the blood and the cross are tucked away for special "discipleship classes."

But these truths are the foundational elements of the gospel; it is preaching these truths that get us to what we call the "good news." Galatians 3:24 says it is the law (or our guilt for breaking it) that brings us to Christ. It's preaching these truths that produce repentance, conversion and true cross-carrying, biblically-modeled, self-sacrificial discipleship.

Unfortunately, many modern pulpits are filled with motivational, self-help talks and some pastors have become little more than life coaches dispensing advice for success and happiness. Much of what we call preaching today is self-help theory and motivational methodology. Leonard Ravenhill said, *"Starving, thirsting people come in and we give them make up, new clothes and a gym membership. We say, 'do these five things and you'll feel better' or 'follow this advice and you'll be fulfilled.' And yet the people are ravenously hungry! We feel good because we think we're offering something of substance but it lacks the power to transform death into life."* Sure, the self-help sermons are covered over with evangelical terms and smattered about with scriptures here and there, but it lacks the quickening, cutting, piercing power that a sharp, two-edged sword should have. To this point, Ravenhill also said, *"Tragically, Hell will be filled with people who've learned from preachers how to be happy and achieve success."*

Saul feared the people. He was afraid that if he upheld the Word of God and demanded obedience to it, they would turn against him. He was afraid they would leave or go find a new king and rationalized: "I don't want to offend anyone; I need to be relational and relevant. If I don't give them what they want, then I might not keep them. Even more, I don't want to appear too demanding or confrontational or make people uncomfortable, I want to be an encourager." But there can be no salvation without repentance, and there can be no repentance without conviction, and there can be no conviction without a preacher preaching the Word of God. Paul said, *"How then shall they call on Him if they've not believed? And how shall they believe if they've not heard? And how shall they hear without a preacher?"* (Romans 10:14).

Sure, we can attract the crowds, and we can keep them coming back for more. But without power of the Word, we are churning out pseudo-converts who may agree intellectually with a few points of theology—they may know something about a virgin birth and another something about Easter—but they cannot endure sound doctrine, cannot tolerate repentance, and cannot handle the call to the cross, because they are accustomed to a soothing gospel that itches their ears.

LEADERS ARE EXAMPLES

Hebrews 13:7 says, *"Obey those who rule over you, and be submissive, for they watch out for your souls, as those who must give account."* James 3:1 warns, *"My brethren, let not many of you become teachers, knowing that we shall receive a stricter judgment."* When Samuel discovered the people's rebellion, he didn't rebuke the people, he rebuked their leader. God will hold the leaders accountable for the condition of their followers because the character of the leader largely influences the character of those that follow him.

Why do people falter in their faith? It is because leaders who lack conviction produce followers who lack conviction.

Without leaders clearly and boldly demonstrating a love for God with all their heart, soul, and strength, followers become confused by blurred standards and a plethora of opinionated questions: "Should I go to church? Should I witness? Should I lift my hands? Should I go to the altar? What is right and what is wrong? Should I read my bible, pray, and fast?" Churches lacking forceful leadership risk returning to the days of Judges when *"there was no king in Israel and everyone did what was right in his own eyes"* (Judges 21:25). Without a Saul to stand up and say, "Watch me, I'll show you how to obey, how to worship, how to serve, how to love and how to give," the body of Christ will continue to waver between the opinions of fervor and frigidity, unresponsive to the call of God.

Why are people unresponsive? Because they watch the leader, infected by the spirit of Saul, sitting across from them and say, "Why should I? The leader isn't doing it." And they are right. Why should followers be inspired to worship when their leaders sit unresponsive with arms crossed in the back of the church? Why should they run to the altar to seek more of God when leaders yawn at their watches dreaming of a football game? Why should followers go to prayer meetings or revival services when most of the leaders don't go? If the leaders don't have a hunger for God, how can those who follow them? Lukewarmness in a church can always be traced back to lukewarmness in the leaders.

"We need you to lead" is the cry from the pew. "We need you to show us how to worship, how to pray, how to serve, and how to love Jesus. We need you to show up for church more than twice a month and show us how to be bold witnesses and fervent prayer warriors. We need you to model this thing called 'discipleship' and show us how to love, how to live, and how to die."

No authority understood this need for strong leadership in

the church more than Paul. In 1 Timothy 4:12, he wrote to the young leader, *"Be an example to the believers in word, in conduct, in love, in spirit, in faith, in purity."* In Philippians 3:17 he said, *"Brethren, join in following my example...as you have us for a pattern"* and, in 1 Thessalonians 1:6, he said, *"You became followers of us and of the Lord."* Paul believed leaders to be a crucial force in the body of Christ setting the standard of godly excellence and pulling others up to it.

LEADERS ARE DELIBERATE

Where Saul failed to lead, Samuel had no hesitation. 1 Samuel 15:32-33: *"Then Samuel said, 'Bring Agag king of the Amalekites here to me.' So Agag came to him cautiously. And Agag said, 'Surely the bitterness of death is past.' But Samuel said, 'As your sword has made women childless, so shall your mother be childless among women.' And Samuel hacked Agag in pieces before the LORD in Gilgal."*

God wants leaders who are deliberate. Deliberate leaders don't apologize for their convictions or fade into the background when resistance arises. Deliberate leaders stand alone among peers and refuse to be influenced by the prevailing attitudes of mediocrity. They believe it is their responsibility to set the standard even if it means being unpopular or even rejected. They see themselves, not as committee members or politicians, nor as everybody's friend—they see themselves as leaders.

Deliberate leadership springs out of an ownership of responsibility. These men and women understand that they're not another face in the crowd; they have a duty to stand apart as an example. The way they talk is intentional, their reactions are deliberate, the things they do, the places they go, the way they worship all have a purpose: to boldly demonstrate how disciples of Christ should live their lives. J. Oswald Sanders indicates this when he wrote in *Spiritual Leadership*, "*The man of leadership caliber will work while others waste time, study while others sleep, pray while others play. There will be no place for loose or lazy habits in word or thought, deed or dress. He will observe a soldierly discipline, diet and deportment, so that he may wage a good warfare.*"[1]

What will cause halfhearted believers to become self-denying disciples? Is it a reminder in the bulletin that workers are needed in the Sunday School? No, it is a leader standing in the place of selfless sacrifice calling people to that same level.

What will cause timid and discouraged saints to stand boldly in the market place as witnesses of the Faith? Is it the latest book written by some distant author telling stories about people we've never met? No, it is a leader out on the streets himself, pounding the pavements, searching for lost souls, pulling converts into the Kingdom and challenging his followers to do the same.

What will cause complacent Christians to intensify their love for God and renounce all idols? Is it a well-written sermon delivered with expository prowess? No, it is a leader visibly demonstrating a passion for God with hands held high and tears streaming down his cheeks in an act of worship. It is a leader who, while enduring secular employ, will not allow his employ to tyrannize his life or push God into the background. It is a leader who will not be dominated by overtime, extracurricular activities, television programs, or family opinions. A determined leader visibly demonstrates the scripture that defines true spirituality: "*As for me and my house, we will serve the Lord*" (Joshua 24:15).

WHAT ARE WE DUPLICATING?

Scriptures demonstrate that the spirit of a leader is imparted to and manifested in the spirit of his or her followers, whether good or bad. David's gallant spirit transformed a mob of bitter and worthless men into a formidable army of warriors. Joshua elevated a multitude of complaining Israelites into a victorious nation. Jesus took common, everyday men and forged them into world changers. On the other hand, when people come under feeble authorities such as Saul, they sink into the same spirit of compromise and malaise imparted to them by that leader. In fact, in Saul's next battle he is found hiding in his tent from Goliath. The people, following his example, take to hiding in their tents as well.

Jesus called us to make disciples. The essence of discipleship is duplicating what we are in others. Hence, we cannot make disciples unless we become disciples. What are we really reproducing? Are we making disciples who know how to crucify themselves and live for others? Or have we created an environment where it is easy for people to call themselves "Christian" yet never truly die to self? Have we (like Saul) fostered an atmosphere where "disciples" can disregard the Word of God while never grieving over their indifference?

Leaders determine the culture of the community whether they intend to or not. The Sauls among us will foster a culture where the lukewarm can remain comfortable in their lack of spirituality. There will be no pressure for them to change. They can keep their sin, ignore the altar, hide from worship, hate their brother, let Agag live, keep the sheep, and never feel badly about it. Saul won't bother them or challenge their complacency. In fact, he'll follow along.

Deliberate leaders, however, foster a climate in which compromisers and carnal Christians could never be comfortable—as they should not be. If Nadab and Abihu were killed for defilement, if Uzzah was cursed for presumption, and Ananias and Saphiria were judged because of pretention, then saints with secret sins should at least feel the discomfort of conviction in God's house on Sunday.

Several years ago, I was alarmed by the blatant rebellion of a man in my church who was committing adultery against his wife, destroying the faith of his children, and ignoring an ultimatum I gave him to either repent or leave the church. Despite the sin he and I both knew he was in, he stood there during worship one Sunday with his hands upraised, smiling and "worshiping" God. I left my seat on the platform, walked directly to him, tapped him on the shoulder, escorted him from the service and rebuked him for his blatant rebellion against the Word of God, his wife, his children, and the church. I killed his Agag. Sadly, he left the church and eventually moved to another state with the woman he impregnated.

There is something wrong when "believers" can walk defiantly in "the lust of the eyes, the lust of the flesh, and the pride of life" and sing praise songs in our services feeling happy and blessed. I don't want "sinning saints" to be able to sit comfortably under my ministry. If I really am a leader, a discipler of believers, then I want there to be a pull, a sense of urgency that stirs compromisers to repentance and makes them hungry for God. I want sinners to feel pressured to change—a pressure that springs out of the intensity of my passion for His presence. I want to foster a culture that makes hunger for God the norm and apathy toward God taboo. While we want the lost to know that God's love accepts them, we should never deceive them into thinking they can follow Him on their own terms.

Unlike Saul, true leaders are not interested in just making people happy, winning friends, or having a large following. Don't be deceived by numbers. Jesus often had crowds following Him and all they wanted was free food. They cared not for Christ, nor grieved over sin, nor intended to carry a cross. We must not convince ourselves that we are good leaders simply because we have a crowd. In fact, Christlike leadership is never impressed with a large following—Christlike leadership is impressed only with the quality of that following. Rick Warren, author of *The Purpose Driven Church*, said, "*The size of a church is not the issue. You can be big and healthy, or big and flabby. You can be small and healthy, or small and wimpy. Big isn't better; small isn't better. Healthy is better. There is no correlation between the size of a church and the strength of a church.*"[2] The issue is not how many people are sitting in the pews; the issue is how many people are denying self, carrying their cross daily and living Christ-centered, God-glorifying lives.

ANY SAUL CAN BUILD A CROWD, BUT ONLY LEADERS PRODUCE DISCIPLES

Jesus was never interested in having a big following. Jesus was interested in disciples who understood how to deny themselves, take up their cross and follow Him. He knew the strength of the church laid in the willingness of His followers to lay down their lives for the gospel. In Luke 14:25, multitudes followed Christ. If Jesus only wanted a large following, He would have organized His team of twelve into a ministry team serving everyone's needs and providing fun programs. But He didn't. Instead, He turned to the crowd and demanded, *"If anyone comes to me and does not hate his father and mother, wife and children, brothers and sisters, yes, and his own life also, he cannot be My disciple."* The Lord ensured the integrity of His follower's commitment, so He challenged them to discipleship.

The Sauls among us do not understand that the church's survival depends on its ability to make disciples. Disciples are the ones who win converts, support missions, labor sacrificially, pay tithes, and even make more disciples. If the church universal, or any local church, is to survive, it will be because of the support and sacrifice of the disciples within it. Unfortunately, Saul doesn't make disciples. Rather than producing a disciplined army with a denying self and fighting God's battles, Saul fosters a spirit of self-serving that views the church as a place to have one's needs met and achieve self-fulfillment.

A recent *Newsweek* article illustrated Saul's broad influence. The report detailed a dramatic new interest in religion, however, *"unlike earlier religious revivals, the aim this time is support, not salvation, help rather than holiness, a circle of spiritual equals rather than an authoritative church or guide. A group affirmation of self is at the top of the agenda which is why some of the least demanding churches are now in the greatest demand."*[3] This reflects a dangerous reality in the church today: too many are interested in a church that makes them feel comfortable rather than a church that makes them into followers of Christ.

Increasingly, people are demanding religious systems that meet their need for spiritual fulfillment without the sacrifices and commitment that true Christianity requires. Ask people what they look for in a church and you will hear responses such as: "sermons that encourage me, uplifting fellowship, good music, kids' programs," or something as simple as "I want it to make me feel good." There was a time when people chose a church on the basis of its ability to disciple them or reveal the deeper truths of God's Word—but not now. People are no longer interested in how God requires them to live; all they want to know is "what's in it for me?"

The reason why this attitude has become so predominate in the church is due largely in part to the spirit of Saul in our leaders. Instead of challenging self-centeredness, Saul caters to it by providing a non-confrontational, "I'm OK, you're OK" atmosphere within the body. When leadership seeks to maintain its own comfort zone, then a comfort zone mentality prevails throughout the church. People are not urged to take up a cross because the leaders don't carry one. Converts are not challenged to put off their self-centered ways because leaders have not put off theirs. The end result of Saul's regime no longer resembles a church that pulls people into intimacy with God, but a social club that pampers personal preferences of immature spiritual babes.

AGAG MUST DIE

In his book, *Bad Religion – How We Became a Nation of Heretics*, Ross Douthat writes: *"America's problem is not too much religion, or too little of it. It's bad religion: the slow motion collapse of traditional Christianity and the rise of a variety of destructive pseudo-Christianities in its place."* Indeed, the concern is not that churches are declining. In fact, many are growing. The concern is that what we are perpetuating is a self-styled, dumbed-down version of the gospel in which Scripture is little more than a refrigerator magnet, the Holy Spirit is a warm fuzzy, Jesus is a life coach, and the Father exists to affirm how special, unique, and wonderful we are.

This is what happens when Saul stands behinds the pulpit and refuses to slaughter the Agags to whom so many are attached. This is what happens when leaders avoid raising the bold standard of God's Word for fear that the people will turn against them and leave. The result is a church of pseudo-converts who think they are saved based on the pretense that we can serve God and do as we please.

It's time to confront the spirit of Saul in the church today. It's time to slay the Agags and slaughter the sheep and lead the people into full obedience of the Word of God. Will some people reject this standard? Certainly! Will some people leave and find another king to follow? You can count on it. But the people who stay will be those who are serious. There may only be twelve of them. But with twelve disciples, sold out for Christ, you can turn the world upside down!

How The Mighty Have Fallen

So when Samuel rose early in the morning to meet Saul, it was told Samuel, saying, "Saul went to Carmel, and indeed, he set up a monument for himself; and he has gone on around, passed by, and gone down to Gilgal."
1 Samuel 15:12

So Samuel said, "When you were little in your own eyes, were you not head of the tribes of Israel? And did not the LORD anoint you king over Israel?"
1 Samuel 15:17

LESSON FIVE

SAUL TURNED HIS MINISTRY INTO A MONUMENT

"To be proud is to pick a fight with God."
Mark Driscoll

A monument is a structure built to memorialize greatness. It calls attention to the significant accomplishments of some person in a way that his or her importance is commemorated into posterity.

In Washington D.C., there exists such a structure. The Washington Monument is both the world's highest stone structure and the world's tallest obelisk, standing over 555 feet or 169 meters. It was completed in 1884 and continues to give tribute to one of America's foremost historical leaders, George Washington.[1]

He was born in 1732 and died in 1799. Hailed as the father of his country, and the leader who was "first in war, first in peace, and first in the hearts of his countrymen," George Washington was the dominant military and political leader of the United States from 1775 to 1797. He led the American victory over Great Britain in the American Revolutionary War, presided over the writing of the U.S. Constitution in 1787, and was the unanimous choice of the electorate to serve as the first American President. Under his leadership, the United States became a strong and financially secure nation that earned the respect of the world.[2] Perhaps no other American historical figure is hailed as having contributed more to this nation's heritage than George Washington and the erection of this monument is a well-deserved commemoration of his greatness.

But imagine for a moment something that never happened. Imagine that George Washington, himself, proposed the idea of this monument to honor his achievements. Pretend for a moment that it was he who commissioned a designer, raised a workforce, and allocated funds for the project. Picture in your mind: George Washington standing before the masses, delivering a speech that recounted all his accomplishments, listed the reasons why he was so great, and then explained how a 555-foot-high obelisk bearing his name in the middle of the capital city would be a fitting tribute to commemorate his glory.

Such a scenario would be outrageous. But this is exactly what King Saul did for himself. In 1 Samuel 15:12, the prophet Samuel came early in the day looking for the king. To his astonishment, he was told that Saul had gone to Gilgal to *"set up a monument for himself."*

What does it mean that he "set up a monument for himself?" It meant that, in the king's mind, Israel was no longer a nation set apart to worship, honor and exalt God in the earth. Instead, Israel was a tribute to Saul, to his abilities, to his great accomplishments. People would look at the monument and immediately think of Saul and what he did for Israel. It didn't matter that Israel had been created by God as a testament to His own glory (Isaiah 46:13). For Saul, the nation of Israel and all that it had become was all about him and his greatness as a leader. Saul had turned his ministry into a monument.

HOW TO PICK A FIGHT WITH GOD

James 4:6 warns us that *"God resists the proud."* Simply stated, to be proud is to pick a fight with God.[3]

"My glory I will not give to another!" is the bold decree of God in Isaiah 42:8. When Saul raised that monument to himself, he was taking the glory that belonged to God. Pride picks a fight with God. It provokes God to defend His glory and put man in his place by humiliating him in failure and defeat. Proverbs 8:13 says the Lord hates *"Pride and arrogance."* As well, Proverbs 16:18 says *"Pride goes before destruction and a haughty spirit before a fall."* This was a lesson Saul was about to learn. Nothing brings blessing from God like humility and nothing brings His judgment like pride.

Saul didn't start out as a monument builder. When the call of God first came to Saul, he was a humble man. He was so contrite and filled with meekness that when chosen to become Israel's king, he hid himself hoping to avoid the appointment (1 Samuel 10:22). At first, Saul was not ruled by ambition or blinded by pride. He understood his inadequacies and knew that in his own strength, he could never lead a nation.

However, after being crowned with authority and anointing, Saul started to change. The taste of success, the sense of power over thousands, the flattery attached to status and privilege all served to inflate his ego with a perverted sense of importance. Rather than seeing himself as a servant to the people, he believed the people existed to serve his great ambitions. Sadly, this humble farm boy who felt too inadequate to lead became so convinced of his own importance that he raised a monument to commemorate his "greatness" (1 Samuel 15:12).

In this we see a subtle danger that resides within gaining authority and anointing. It's the tendency to think, "Because I am the leader, because I have the vision and the anointing, and because I am the one out in front, I am, therefore, the important one, the more significant one, the essential person in the organization, even more important than those who serve under me." It is an unspoken, often subconscious feeling, but it often effects how we talk to and treat those around us. It is nothing more than pride. The dark, ugly, spiritual cancer we call pride. It spreads and metastasizes. It controls and corrupts and changes us into tyrants denying the humility of servanthood and turning our ministry into a monument to show off our own greatness.

A FELLOWSHIP OF MONUMENT BUILDERS

But is Saul really that different from any of us? Don't most of us start out in humility only to have our character corrupted by success and promotion? Don't many of us fall to the subtle entitlements of pride?

Remember how easy it was to be humble when you were the new guy? Remember what it was like when you were just starting out in ministry? More than likely, you were willing to do anything. You could take orders, serve anyone, and do what you were told to do no matter how humiliating and demeaning it might seem to be.

But like Saul, after success sets in and "the new guy" gets promoted, after we gain authority and command over others, it becomes harder for us to take orders and do lowly tasks. Soon we start "realizing" how special and important we are. And now, those menial, insignificant things we used to do unto the Lord are somehow "beneath" us. Sweep the floor? Clean bathrooms? Carry someone's bags? Those are for other people, less important than us. Now we have staff that does the sweeping and an entourage to carry our bags. As "Anointed Men of God" with powerful ministries, we think we need only to be concerned about those tasks that are "worthy" of our precious time and attention. And so begins the building of our monuments.

Have you made any monuments lately? Has ministry become about you? Consider a few examples of those who had the privilege to lead but succumbed to the subtle entitlements of pride.

JAMES AND JOHN:
SEEKING AUTHORITY TO GAIN PREEMINENCE

"Grant us that we may sit, one on Your right hand and the other on Your left, in Your glory" (Mark 10:37). James and John had it all wrong. They thought leadership was about getting authority and being in control. For them, ministry was a monument. It was a way to gain power and control over the ones they were leading.

This is how most people think of leadership. They imagine being a great leader with a great reputation that enjoys prestige, privilege, and respect. But Jesus had a different idea about great leadership. He said, *"Whoever desires to become great among you shall be your servant...And whoever of you desires to be first shall be slave of all"* (Mark 10:43-44). To Him, leadership was servanthood and the greatest leaders were those who were willing to serve.

What does it mean to be a servant? It means to give yourself in the service of others. A servant is concerned more with meeting the needs of those he serves than he is with his own needs. James and John, however, were caught up in a worldly attitude regarding leadership. They thought being a leader was about advancing and promoting themselves. It was a monument. To them, it centered around being admired, gaining authority and exercising control over others. Even worse, to the worldly thinker, leadership is often an opportunity to hold others down and use them to fulfill your own personal ambitions.

But in Christ, leadership is the exact opposite. Consider Jesus' response to James' and John's monument building. *"You know that those who are considered rulers over the Gentiles lord it over them, and their great ones exercise authority over them. Yet it shall not be so among you...whoever desires to become great among you shall be your servant and whoever of you desires to be first shall be slave of all."* Christian leadership is not promoting or advancing self; neither is it holding others down to serve you. In Christ, leadership is being more concerned with the needs and welfare of others than you are with your own. We lead, not to be admired, honored or recognized, but out of a love for others. We seek positions only to facilitate ministry. Our motivation is to edify others, to meet the needs of others, to lift up others, and promote them over ourselves.

If we aspire to leadership out of a desire for power, recognition or control, we are aspiring for the wrong reason. Our ministry will be polluted with impure motives and defiled by worldly ambition. What's worse is it will be void of God's blessing and will actually draw down His curse. James 4:6 says, *"God resists the proud."* Proverbs 16:18 tell us that *"Pride goes before destruction, and a haughty spirit before a fall."* Self-promotion provokes God to move against us and pull our ministry down. Humility, on the other hand, invokes God's blessing and rich provision.

SIMON THE SORCERER:
SEEKING ANOINTING TO ACHIEVE SUCCESS

It seemed to be a decent request. He sought the power of the Holy Spirit to make him effective in ministry. In Acts 8:19 Simon said to Peter, *"Give me this power also, that anyone on whom I lay hands may receive the Holy Spirit."*

Is this not the prayer of all who desire to be used of God? Do we all not seek the anointing of the Holy Spirit even as Jesus declared Himself to be anointed of the Holy Spirit? Should not every preacher of the Word be as Paul who yearned for his preaching to be in the demonstration of the Spirit and power?

It would seem to be so for Simon. But Peter's response cut right to the core of what was really in his heart. Peter said, *"Your money perish with you, because you thought that the gift of God could be purchased with money! You have neither part nor portion in this matter, for your heart is not right in the sight of God. Repent therefore of this your wickedness, and pray God if perhaps the thought of your heart may be forgiven you. For I see that you are poisoned by bitterness and bound by iniquity"* (Acts 8:20-23).

Not everyone who desires the anointing desires it for the right reasons. Some seek anointing because it makes their ministry into a monument. It is a means for recognition and respect.

This is largely true in Pentecost where we have elevated anyone with an anointing to celebrity status. In other words, the anointing has become a commodity that will open doors, give you respect, and provide your ministry with wider appeal. As a result, many, like Simon, desire the anointing for the allure and admiration and great acclamation it brings from the crowds. It's true—just study our contemporary history.

Whether it's Brownsville or Lakeland or Toronto, anointed preachers attract great crowds, anointed leaders have huge followings, anointed people are regarded as exceptional, extraordinary, and even somewhat superior. This is what Simon understood and what many modern preachers now know: with anointing, there will be fame, success, and usually large amounts of money.

Indeed we need the Holy Spirit for effective ministry but we must check our motives. Do I seek the anointing so that people can be edified or do I seek anointing so I can be admired? Do I pray and fast for Holy Spirit unction so God can be glorified in me or so I can look good in the pulpit and sound good to the pew? Do I want anointing to draw applause, get more "amens" and attract a bigger crowd?

Anytime an altar call is given for more unction, we ought to run forward like a starving man chasing a meal. But let us be careful of our motives. Too many seek the power of God for personal reasons like Simon. They're like a man in a huge car driving up to a gas pump saying, "Fill it up with the highest octane you have. I got a big engine and I want to hear it roar." We think the Holy Ghost is power for our ministries, supplying fuel to make us better, stronger, faster, and more effective. But the Holy Ghost is not going to be a means to anyone's end. The purpose of the anointing is only to bring glory to God, not recognition to man. Any motive to bring glory, recognition, or acclaim to man is nothing more than Simon looking for more sorcery so he could seduce the crowd.

LUCIFER THE ANGEL:
SEEKING GLORY TO BE ADMIRED

"How you are fallen from heaven, O Lucifer, son of the morning! How you are cut down to the ground, you who

weakened the nations! For you have said in your heart: 'I will ascend into heaven, I will exalt my throne above the stars of God; I will also sit on the mount of the congregation on the farthest sides of the north; I will ascend above the heights of the clouds, I will be like the Most High'"* (Isaiah 14:12-14).

Because of certain descriptions of his being that include musical ability connected to worship and leadership, some theologians speculate that Lucifer was the worship leader in heaven. Unfortunately, instead of directing worship to God, he diverted it from God and unto himself. He turned his ministry into a monument.

He said, *"I will ascend into heaven, I will exalt my throne above the stars of God; I will also sit on the mount of the congregation"* (Isaiah 14:13). For Lucifer, ministry was all about him. He wanted a position, not so he could direct worship to God but divert it to himself. He lusted for attention and admiration; he wanted the focus to be upon his own beauty and special gifts. A longing for respect, recognition, esteem, and praise was the motivator that secretly drove him in his duties. He was not concerned about how much glory God received, he was mostly interested in how much glory he received.

Likewise, the "Lucifers" in leadership today are not concerned about the well-being of the church or the glory of God. They are concerned about how they look, how they are esteemed, and how many people pat them on the back at the end of a service and say, "Wow, you did a great job. What talent you have!" For them, ministry is a monument. It is something to fill their own need for affirmation and acceptance.

Pastors, worship leaders, and ministers beware. We must take heed against such prideful motives. Ministry is not an opportunity to showcase abilities or draw applause of people.

It is not a spotlight to demonstrate how skillfully one can play an instrument, "hit" the high notes, or get the crowd to shout. Ministry is about one thing: bringing glory to God by serving others. Any motive for self-promotion is rooted in the prideful exaltation of Lucifer and is an unacceptable offering of ministry.

TEAR DOWN THOSE MONUMENTS

In our attempt to tear down the idols of self in our ministry monuments, it is important not to swing the pendulum too far in the opposite direction. Some, in their attempt to act humble, have actually taken on what the Bible calls a "False Humility"—which is actually a more dangerous and subtle form of pride.

Humility is defined as an unassuming or moderate estimation of one's abilities or achievements in relationship to one's own importance. Paul called it a "lowliness of mind" that enables one to "esteem others better than himself" and "not think of himself more highly than he ought to think" (Philippians 2:3, Romans 12:3).

Indeed humility is one of the most important virtues for it demonstrates not only one's ability to overcome prideful impulses, but also his inner dependence on God. For this reason God has promised to *"give grace to the humble"* and *"lift him up"* (James 4:6, 10).

Let us cast off the spirit of King Saul. Let us tear down these monuments we have built to our own greatness and seek rather to put all focus, all attention and all glory on the King of Kings and Lord of our lives. *"Not unto us, O LORD, not unto us, but to Your name give glory, because of Your mercy, because of Your truth"* (Psalm 115:1).

How The Mighty Have Fallen

"Then he stood and cried out to the armies of Israel, and said to them, 'Why have you come out to line up for battle? Am I not a Philistine, and you the servants of Saul? Choose a man for yourselves, and let him come down to me. If he is able to fight with me and kill me, then we will be your servants. But if I prevail against him and kill him, then you shall be our servants and serve us.' And the Philistine said, 'I defy the armies of Israel this day; give me a man, that we may fight together.' When Saul and all Israel heard these words of the Philistine, they were dismayed and greatly afraid."

1 Samuel 17:8-11

LESSON SIX

SAUL SURRENDERED TO A SPIRIT OF FEAR

"A leader once convinced that a particular course of action is the right one, must remain firm and undaunted when the going gets tough."

Ronald Reagan

The true quality of a leader is revealed when he is confronted by a Goliath.

Almost any leader can develop a vision and lay out a strategy for achieving it. Almost any leader can recruit people, motivate workers and supervise a team. The real test of leadership comes, however, when that leader faces obstacles. When resistance rises and adversity threatens success—when challenges loom as insurmountable—what does the leader do? Does he hesitate? Is he intimidated? Does he second guess and back peddle or does he remain firm and undaunted when the going gets tough?

The duty of leadership is to confront status quo and pull the people to a better place. Rosalynn Carter, wife of former U.S. President Jimmy Carter, said, "A leader takes people where they want to go. A great leader takes people where they don't necessarily want to go but where they ought to be." In the course of such an act, a leader will undoubtedly face resistance. "Goliath-sized" obstacles will rise to challenge both the leader's vision and his resolve. How a person responds to Goliath reveals if he or she is a true leader, or just a custodian sporting a fancy title.

Saul had a title, but that didn't make him a leader. Men may have called him king, but that didn't give him command. Sure, he could organize the infantry for a march and arrange the chariots for a parade, but when it came to the business of battle—the hard work of overcoming obstacles to success—he fell apart. Rather than meeting the antagonist on the battlefield and inspiring his followers forward, he brought the people to a halt and the ranks became stagnate.

Leadership is ten percent vision and ninety percent overcoming the obstacles that hinder the vision. There will always be obstacles. People will always see some giant standing in the way of their progress. It could be a lack of resources, conflict within the organization, or resistance from outsiders. Whatever the obstacle, the leader's job is to stand with confidence against it, plot a course to overcome it, and cheer his followers on to victory.

To the contrary, nothing will destroy the credibility of a leader like a spirit of fear. It wasn't Goliath that paralyzed the Israelite army. They were paralyzed by their own leader who surrendered to fear. King Saul, frightened by Goliath's challenge, retreated from his post and Israel's advance was halted. If he had faith, if he had met the challenge with confidence and courage, his army would have followed him like they followed David. When David entered the scene and demonstrated his faith, the Israelites arose and defeated the Philistines. All they needed was a leader who believed God for success no matter how dire the circumstance.

People need leaders who have faith—even those who are

critical and defiant. They may say, "It can't be done; it's impossible; we don't have the means or resources." But, in reality, they are hoping for a leader who will stand with confidence and say "God is able." They will respond to a leader like young David who declares, "If God is for us who can be against us. Don't give up; we can do all things through Christ who strengthens us."

Therefore, if there was one thing I could pray into the leaders of my church it would not be a new vision, smart ideas, fancy programs, or even great resources. The one thing I would pray into our leaders would be a good attitude—an attitude of faith.

FAITH IS AN ATTRACTIVE ATTITUDE

John Maxwell wrote, *"Many people who approach the area of vision in leadership have it all backward. They believe that if the cause is good enough, people will automatically buy into it and follow. But that's not how leadership really works. People don't at first follow worthy causes. They follow worthy leaders who promote worthwhile causes. People buy into the leader first, then the leader's vision."*

In the early 1900s, the *London Times* reportedly carried an advertisement that read, "Men wanted for hazardous journey. Small wages, bitter cold, long months of complete darkness, constant danger. Safe return doubtful. Honor and recognition in case of success."[1] The man alleged to have run the article was the famed explorer Ernest Shackleton and his vision was to make the first crossing of the perilous Antarctic continent by foot. He was hoping, by use of the controversial article, to recruit twenty six men to make the dangerous journey with him.[2]

Of course, it wasn't a very inspiring vision statement and one might think that no person in his right mind would respond to such an uninspiring help wanted ad. However, historian Julian Watkins reported that over five thousand people applied for the job.[3] Why such a positive response? Because in London at that time, Ernest Shackleton was a man greatly respected. He was well-reputed as a trustworthy leader and a capable explorer. And, as a man expected to achieve greatness in his lifetime, people wanted to be a part of whatever he was doing. Those five-thousand men were not signing up for a great vision—they signed up for a great leader.[4]

Ernest Shackleton exemplifies an important principle of leadership: people are not attracted to smart programs or good ideas—people are attracted to people. In other words, people don't follow us because they like our vision or are impressed with our plan. They sign up for our vision because they believe in us; they have confidence in the quality and content of our character. This is why powerful advertising firms hire popular personalities and successful athletes to promote their products. When people feel good about the presenting individual, they buy into their product—or vision. For example, people buy Nike sneakers, not because they necessarily like the shoes, but because they've bought into Michael Jordan. Once people buy into someone, they will give his or her vision a chance. Therefore, before you ask people to buy into your vision, you need to ask, "Do people buy into you?"

King David attracted many followers. In 1 Samuel 22, we see him living in the cave of Adullam. He's been branded a fugitive by Saul, considered a traitor to the nation and is being hunted like an animal. One would think that no one would want to be associated with him, let alone follow him as a leader. Yet Verse 2 says, "*...everyone who was in distress, everyone who was in debt, and everyone who was discontented* *gathered to him. So he became captain over them. And there were about four hundred men with him."*

What was it that drew so many people to this outcast leader? Did people follow David because he had a great vision? Did people flock to him because he gave them such promise for their future? Of course not—he was living in a cave, being hunted by the king, acting insane to avoid punishment from the Philistines. Yet hundreds came to him. Why? Because there was something about the man—something about his spirit, his disposition, his attitude.

In Psalm 57 this attitude is revealed. While running from Saul and living in caves, at the lowest point of his life, David writes songs of praise in which he declares his confidence in God's deliverance. His spirit never wavered. He never grew discouraged. He never complained or succumbed to fear. That's what those four-hundred despots saw. They saw the way he kept singing praise songs and the way he rejoiced in the Lord. They saw his confidence and optimism despite the gloom of the cave and sentence of death upon him. They came to him because of his spirit—not his vision. They came to him because he inspired them; he encouraged them and made them feel better about themselves.

Faith, optimism, confidence: these are the attitudes people are attracted to. If a leader is going to build a following, then he needs to demonstrate these qualities.

Former president of the United States, Ronald Reagan—one America's greatest leaders and foremost optimists—often told a joke about twin boys about five or six years old. Their parents were worried that the boys had developed extreme personalities: one was a total pessimist and the other a total optimist. To allay their concerns, the parents took their sons to a psychiatrist. First the psychiatrist treated the pessimist. Trying to brighten his outlook, the doctor took him to a room piled to the ceiling with brand new toys. But instead of yelping with delight, the little boy burst into tears. "What's the matter?" the doctor asked, baffled. "Don't you want to play with any of the toys?" "Of course," the little boy bawled, "but if I did I'd only break them and get into trouble." Next the psychiatrist treated the optimist. Trying to dampen his ridiculously positive outlook, the psychiatrist took him to a room piled to the ceiling with horse manure. But instead of wrinkling his nose in disgust, the optimist shouted in delight, clambered to the top of the pile, dropped to his knees, and began gleefully digging out scoop after scoop with his bare hands. "What do you think you're doing?" the psychiatrist asked, just as baffled by the optimist as he had been by the pessimist. "With all this manure," the little boy replied, beaming, "there must be a pony in here somewhere!"

Presidential Advisor Edwin Meese recalled that "Ronald Reagan told this joke so often that it got to be kind of a joke with the rest of the staff. Whenever something would go wrong, somebody on the staff would be sure to say, "There must be a pony in here somewhere."[5]

This is the kind of spirit people are attracted to. The spirit that says, no matter what kind of difficulties life throws at us, there are sure to be benefits buried in there somewhere. It is the kind of attitude that refuses fear, refuses to believe that something bad will happen, refuses to say, "We can't do it. Goliath is too big, the giants are too many, we don't have enough resources or money or people; if we try, we will fail."

For this reason, when God calls a leader, the first thing He commands him is "fear not!" At Joshua's coronation, the Lord said, *"...be strong and very courageous...do not be afraid, nor be dismayed, for the LORD your God is with you wherever you go"* (Joshua 1:5-9). One of the most important qualities that God looks for in people who lead is the ability to demonstrate faith over fear—to believe God for success in the face of seemingly insurmountable odds.

FEAR IS A CONTAGIOUS POISON

Attitudes are contagious and bad attitudes are more contagious than good ones. It is easy to be infected by someone's sickness but nearly impossible to catch their good health. The same is true of attitude. Fear spreads quickly. Unabated, it spreads like wildfire gaining more momentum with each person it infects.

Saul's reaction to Goliath shows us the worst thing a leader can do. He hid himself away, afraid to confront the issue, unable to rally the troops with faith, optimism and a "can-do" attitude. As a result, fear spread throughout the camp like a virus devouring it's victim.

The same dynamic occurred in Numbers 13 when the spies returned from the land of Canaan with a bad report. Although God promised them victory, they complained, *"'The land through which we have gone as spies is a land that devours its inhabitants, and all the people whom we saw in it are men of great stature. There we saw the giants...and we were like grasshoppers in our own sight, and so we were in their sight.' So all the congregation lifted up their voices and cried, and the people wept that night"* (Numbers 13:32-14:1). Despite the fiery words of encouragement delivered by Joshua and Caleb, the dire prediction of the spies spread like an infectious disease throughout the camp. Such is the effect that fear has on a group of people.

Faith and fear are opposite twins. Faith is the expectation that something good will happen. Fear is also expectation, but it expects that something bad will happen. It is an attitude of discouragement that says, "We can't. Goliath is too big, the giants are too many, we don't have enough resources or money or people; if we try, we will fail." This is the attitude that most people will take. When the twelve spies surveyed the land in Numbers 10, it was the majority who feared the giants and said, "It can't be done; we'll be defeated." Anytime a vision is pursued, there will be those whose natural expectation is the worst. There will always be those pessimists who focus on the negative, who see the potential for failure and retreat because of it. But God is looking for leaders. People who can see the possibilities, expect the best and challenge the attitudes of fear.

Bruce Wilkinson wrote, "As God's chosen, blessed sons and daughters we are expected to attempt something (so large) that failure is guaranteed—unless God steps in." Have you ever been in a place where you felt that the task before you was too far beyond your ability to meet it? Have you ever felt that unless God shows up, unless God intervenes or provides, I'm going to fail, miserably? It is called "dependence" and it is exactly where we are supposed to be living. It is a difficult place, a challenging place, an uncomfortable place, but it is where God expects us, as leaders, to be. In fact, He has a label for it; it's called "Walking by Faith!"[6]

Noah called it building an ark, even though it had never even rained. Moses called it crossing the wilderness, without food, water, and adequate preparation. Abraham called it sacrificing Isaac when Isaac was his only hope for an inheritance. Joshua called it marching around Jericho. David called it confronting Goliath. Shadrach, Meshach, and Abed-Nego called it refusing to bow down. And Peter called it walking on the water.

What do you call it? What ark are you building, what wilderness are you crossing, what Isaac are you sacrificing, what Jericho are you facing, what Goliath are you challenging, what water are you thinking about walking on? Or, are you living a life safely within the comfy, cozy walls of a boat.

Let's be clear: the feeling that you can't do it—that this is beyond you, that you're in over your head—is exactly what you're supposed to be feeling. If you're not feeling that, then chances are you're hiding with Saul in the tent. If you're not feeling that, then Goliath has already won. You've refused to dream something beyond your ability. You've rejected the vision that God has to do something so incredible, so miraculous, that only He can get the glory. If you're not feeling that, then you are not leading where God wants you to be leading.

Too many leaders are reclining back in their tents, saying, "Well thank God. I'm saved. Thank God our bills are paid and we have a happy little church. Thank God I get a paycheck and we have no problems." That's not leading, that's just managing, that's status quo. Leaders, by nature, pick fights. They upset the equilibrium that everyone else in the organization is looking for. They challenge status quo and force people to see things, not as they are, but as God wants them to be. They force people out of comfortable tents and make them realize there's a Goliath in the camp. They address the brutal facts and set things right. If you don't do that, you're not a leader, you're a tent dweller.

God is looking for some people who are willing to do some "moving and shaking" for the Kingdom of God. There are already too many timid soldiers hiding in their tents afraid to take on Goliaths. God is looking for some Davids to step out and say, "I'm willing to believe God to do something incredible."

It's not about your ability, your education, your income bracket, it is about your faith. Can you believe God to show up, provide, or do something incredible? Can you believe God to tear down walls, topple giants, move mountains, and deliver you through a burning fiery furnace so the smell of smoke is not even on you?

LEADERS PICK FIGHTS WITH GIANTS

In Matthew 14, Jesus told his disciples to feed the five thousand. The disciples said, *"We don't have the resources. We only have five fish and two loaves. Send them to the village where the resources are."* That's how we usually work. Typically, we wait until we have resources in hand and then say, "OK, now we can trust God." But that's not trusting God—that's doing it in the flesh and relying on our own ability. And if it's your ability and your resources, who gets the glory when it's done? You!

But God wants to do something so incredible, so out of the box, so awesome, that after it's done the only response can be: "See what God has done! No man could not have done it." That's why he chooses the foolish things, the weak things, and the base things of this world; so no flesh can glory in His sight.

In December 2007, the American economy fell into what is now known as the Great Recession. It is generally acknowledged to be the most devastating global economic crisis since the Great Depression. As a result, the United States lost more than 7.5 million jobs, and the unemployment rate doubled—peaking at more than 10 percent. The collapse of the housing and equity market destroyed trillions of dollars in personal wealth and made the overwhelming majority of Americans financially insecure as millions lost their homes in foreclosures and bankruptcies.

Not the least to feel this economic decline were churches and non-profits. The *Wall Street Journal* reported that contributions to charities including religious organizations dropped by 20 to 30 percent since 2008 and remain at all-time lows. Many churches have been forced to reduce staff, eliminate programs, and even close their doors.[7]

This is the kind of Goliath many leaders face today. Not a nine-foot-high warrior clad in armor, but an average donor who struggles to support the ministry in hard financial times.

But this is when leaders need to lead. We cannot hide in our tents and hope the giant goes away—we must get out in front. Frame the discussion in words of faith and remind everyone that God is still, and always will be, able!

It was in 2008, just as the recession was beginning to ripple through the country, that our church was developing plans to launch a capital stewardship campaign for the expansion of our facilities. We were proposing to build a $4 million project in a climate of financial uncertainty, unemployment, and great emotional distress. Some in our leadership team questioned the wisdom of moving forward, believing the project to be doomed by this economic Goliath. But other leaders, including myself, remained undaunted.

I told our leadership team and our church, now is not the time to draw back. Now is not the time to put the vision on hold, hide in our tents and retreat back in fear. If God is in this vision, which we knew He was, we must trust that He will provide. So we forged ahead. Many of us made sacrificial pledges. Some did not—some even dropped out of the campaign—but those who did saw miracles. In fact, my wife and I paid off our pledge eight months ahead of time, as did our campaign director. God was doing something that only He could get the glory for. By the end of the campaign, amidst a struggling economy, our church giving increased substantially and we were able to allocate an amount to savings each month that far exceeded what we would need for the monthly payments on the mortgage. Not only would we be able to build, we would pay off the mortgage well ahead of our amortization schedule. To God be the glory!

People who achieve greatness think differently than the rest of us. They talk differently, they pray differently, they look at challenges differently. To the man or woman who achieves greatness, challenges are not hindrances, they are opportunities for God to demonstrate His greatness on our behalf. When most of us look at five loaves and two fishes, we see little more than a kid's lunch and don't even think of meeting people's needs. But people of greatness see the beginnings of a huge banquet feast. When most of us see a woman at the well who's had five husbands and a boyfriend she's living with, we see a dysfunctional, damaged individual. But, people of faith and greatness see a potentially powerful witness who can testify of God's redeeming grace. When most of us see a band of four-hundred miserable, distressed, indebted malcontents, we see undesirables, social rejects. But David, a man of faith and greatness, saw the makings of a great army that would establish a nation.

Imagine Caleb walking back from the recon mission with those ten spies. He can't stop talking about what he saw. He's so excited about it, he's animated and almost giddy with joy. He says to the others, "Did you see it? Did you see the fruit, the milk and honey? Did you see the flowing streams, the lush fields, the beauty? And did you see that one glorious mountain? That's what I want. I'm going to ask Moses..." Interrupting him, the spies retort, "All we saw were giants, walled cities and impossibilities." Caleb says, "Giants, what giants? Oh you mean those big guys? Those aren't giants, those are my future servants. And those cities, those are my cities. I'm not afraid, God is able and He will deliver them into our hands."

GET OUT OF THE TENT!

The time has come for us to abandon the safety of the tent

and move into a place where we are dependent on the provision of God to keep us secure. The time has come for us to be leaders who don't just talk about miracles, divine provision, and glorifying God. The time has come for us to experience miracles and get some of our own testimonies of divine provision. But that can only happen if we kick that cowardly Saul out of the tent and pick a fight with Goliath.

How The Mighty Have Fallen

So the women sang as they danced, and said: "Saul has slain his thousands, And David his ten thousands. Then Saul was very angry, and the saying displeased him; and he said, "They have ascribed to David ten thousands, and to me they have ascribed only thousands. Now what more can he have but the kingdom?" So Saul eyed David from that day forward. And it happened on the next day that the distressing spirit from God came upon Saul, and he prophesied inside the house. So David played music with his hand, as at other times; but there was a spear in Saul's hand. And Saul cast the spear, for he said, "I will pin David to the wall!" But David escaped his presence twice.

1 Samuel 18:7-11

LESSON SEVEN

SAUL WAS THREATENED BY OTHER LEADERS

"Now what more can he have but the kingdom?"

King Saul

No matter who you are or how great your success, there will always come another who seems to be better, smarter, and more talented. But what do you do when that person is one of your own workers? And what do you do when the people in your church or organization praise and admire him or her more than they do you?

Young David had accomplished an incredible feat. He boldly confronted Goliath and rid Israel of a terrible menace. Through this, he demonstrated his loyalty to God and country as well as his own greatness as a leader. It's not that he made Saul look bad. He simply looked "better" than Saul. He did what Saul could not—or would not do—and all Israel knew it. "Saul has slain his thousands, but David his ten thousands," the women sang as they praised David in a celebration of dance. It would seem, at least it did to Saul, that the people believed David was a better man than him.

So what is a leader to do? How should one react when a subordinate receives more praise and applause then the one in charge? If you are like Saul, the choice is clear. You simply pick up a spear and throw it at him. You ruin that "usurper" before he or she steals your kingdom from you.

Absurd? Outrageous? Indeed, it sounds extreme but this is exactly what many leaders in the Kingdom of God are doing to the aspiring and talented workers under them. Subordinates who take initiative and succeed, whose special gifts and abilities are praised by fellow workers and church members, are often met by the suspicion and resentment of the leaders they serve. Their fear is that these young "Davids" will not only steal their popularity, but they could steal the "kingdom" that the authority believes is his by right.

THE MANDATE OF LEADERSHIP

A leader throwing spears is an offense to kingdom leadership. Imagine Peter being so envious of Paul's success that he forbids him from planting a church. Or picture Paul being so threatened by Timothy's popularity that he spreads rumors about him. Or imagine John the Baptist labeling Jesus a fraud because he is afraid of losing his followers. This is not leadership, it is self preservation. It is not advancing the church for the glory of God; it is expanding an empire for the glory of self.

In the world, leaders aspire to greatness by achieving positions of power and authority. They measure success by the amount of people under their control and the largeness of their popularity. Unfortunately, many "Christian" leaders have come to define greatness in similar terms. To them it is building big churches, commanding huge crowds, and achieving fame. Their attitude is also the same as the world's regarding people—especially subordinates. They are seen as objects to manipulate and control for the leader's own benefit. In fact, followers who show promise or have some better quality than the leader are perceived as threats to be suppressed and are denied opportunity for promotion.

This was a great failure of King Saul just as it is for many church leaders. The mandate of kingdom leadership is to raise others up and release them rather than hold them down and repress them. Ephesians 4:11-12 says apostles, prophets, evangelists, pastors, and teachers are to equip the saints for the work of Christ's ministry, not suppress them for the sake of one's own popularity. Clearly, scripture requires spiritual authorities to identify and prepare potential leaders for future ministry office. Failure to do this is a serious betrayal of leadership. In fact, it is a betrayal of the very mandate given to leaders through the Word of God.

The following are three essential attitudes of leadership that every elder must have to raise leaders. Without them, he or she will succumb to the same fear that gripped King Saul and made him an adversary to the plan of God for His Kingdom. First, one must have a vision greater than one's own. Second, one needs a heart to mentor followers. And third, there must be a willingness to let go of status.

THOSE WHO LEAD MUST HAVE A VISION GREATER THAN THEMSELVES

There are many ministries today named after the men and women who founded them. Some of them are internationally renowned and world reaching, and we thank God for them. But what happens after that man or woman dies? Most likely, the ministry they have built will eventually die with them. Indeed, the ministry may have had an impact, but it was for a limited time and limited generation. Their vision for that ministry was no greater than themselves.

In contrast, Moses is one of the Bible's greatest leaders whose achievements are still impacting the world today. His success remains, not only because he led Israel to the Promised Land, but because he was a leader who raised up other leaders. In Exodus 18:25-26, Moses *"Chose able men out of all Israel, and made them heads over the people: rulers of thousands, rulers of hundreds, rulers of fifties, and rulers of tens. So they judged the people at all times."* Furthermore, in Numbers 11, Moses rejoiced to learn that seventy of his subordinates had received the same anointing he had and prophesied among the people. When others expected him to be threatened and put a stop to it, Moses declared, *"Are you zealous for my sake? Oh, that all the LORD'S people were prophets and that the LORD would put His Spirit upon them!"* Why did Moses have such a passion for raising, training, and releasing leaders? Because he had a vision greater than himself.

Moses understood that his life and the scope of his ministry were limited. God showed him (Numbers 20:12) that his influence would go no further than the banks of the Jordan River (Deuteronomy 34:5). But Moses' vision was unlimited. He wanted more than to merely be a faithful pastor, enlarging his following and securing some property. He had a greater vision; one for a future beyond his grasp, for a land that he would never see and a people he would never meet. Moses knew that to fulfill this vision, he must raise up leaders who could extend his reach into those lands and touch those lives that he could not personally touch. So in Numbers 27, he raised up Joshua, his assistant and choice man (Numbers 11:28), laid hands on him and commissioned him to lead in the regions beyond. As a result, a grand nation was established that would impact the world for centuries to come.

On the contrary, leaders who are threatened by their

apprentices have a weak and limited vision. By suppressing or attacking subordinates they reveal how small-minded and inferior their caliber of leadership truly is. They care only for their specific interests in the here and now and no vision for advancing the Kingdom of God by advancing those He calls.

THOSE WHO LEAD MUST HAVE A HEART TO MENTOR FOLLOWERS

In 2 Timothy 2:2, Paul told Timothy, *"...the things that you have heard from me among many witnesses, commit these to faithful men who will be able to teach others also."* The biblical model of leadership is concerned, not only with influencing the masses, but also on mentoring the few.

Almost every great leader in God's Kingdom was first entrusted to a mentor before released into ministry. Paul had Barnabas and Timothy had Paul. And Timothy, in turn, was instructed to raise up elders in his church. Kingdom leaders must understand the sacred trust they have in recognizing, training, and elevating the aspiring leaders under them. God's plan for preparing, conditioning, and training future pastors, teachers, and missionaries begins with an established leader who is willing to pour himself or herself into up and coming protégés. Those who fail to do so could be preventing the rise of another David or depriving the world of the next great Joshua.

One reason why leaders fail to mentor their subordinates is they fail to fully grasp the potential that their protégé has. The pastor who mentored me never imagined I would carry his impartation throughout India and Africa to thousands of pastors and church leaders. It is very likely that the men and women I am mentoring will double what I do and go twice as far. Never underestimate this. The young man under you could be the next Rienhard Bonnke; the young woman you are coaching could be the next Joyce Meyer.

In 1855, a Sunday School teacher named Edward Kimbell led a 19-year old Boston shoe clerk to Jesus Christ. The shoe clerk's name was Dwight L. Moody and he became a world-renowned evangelist who led hundreds of thousands to Christ in the United States and England. Through D.L. Moody's dynamic preaching, the evangelistic zeal of a local pastor, Frederick B. Meyer, was awakened in 1879. While preaching on a college campus, Pastor Meyer converted a student named J. Wilbur Chapman to Christ. In turn, Chapman engaged in YMCA work and employed a former baseball player, Billy Sunday, to do evangelistic work. Billy Sunday held a revival in Charlotte, North Carolina. Because of this revival, another preacher named Mordecai Ham was brought to town to preach. During Ham's revival, the Holy Spirit began tugging on the heart of a 16 year-old son of a farmer. That 16 year-old boy's name was Billy Graham.

Billy Graham has preached the Gospel in person to more people than any other person in history. It is estimated that more than 3.2 million souls have responded to the invitations to receive Jesus Christ at his crusades. It is further estimated that his lifetime audience, including radio and television broadcasts, topped 2.2 billion.[1]

Impressive to say the least, but it all started with a Sunday School teacher named Edward Kimbell who had a heart to mentor followers. The most valuable leaders in the Kingdom of God are not those who build great buildings or gain large followings—the most valuable leaders are those who are committed to mentor a few. Indeed, it is essential that we preach to the masses and win as many to Christ as we possibly can. But the posterity of the gospel is preserved not in mass evangelism. It is preserved in the few we disciple, the few we train, the few we impart to and ensure the DNA of discipleship is encoded in their spirits for generations to come.

The greatest testimony to one's leadership is the birth of multiple ministries under his or her tutorship. The reason why Saul tried to kill David is that he wanted the success and acclaim that belonged to his apprentice. What he failed to understand was that had he blessed and released David, he would have shared in David's reward. There is great honor in being a mentor and a spiritual father. Jesus said, *"He who receives a prophet in the name of a prophet shall receive a prophet's reward. And he who receives a righteous man in the name of a righteous man shall receive a righteous man's reward"* (Matthew 10:41-42). In other words, those who equip and enable workers for God will share in the rewards they receive for their labors. It's quite possible that when Billy Graham receives his reward for the millions of souls saved, Edward Kimbell, D.L. Moody, and the others who mentored down the line will be standing beside him sharing his reward.

You never know, the next Billy Graham could be sitting in your youth group. Or he may be two or three generations ahead. The point is: get someone ready for ministry. Equip him, encourage him, and mentor him and you will share in that prophet's reward.

THOSE WHO LEAD MUST BE WILLING TO LET GO OF STATUS

John the Baptist said, *"He must increase and I must decrease"* (John 3:30). The crowds were curious that people were being drawn to Jesus and leaving John behind. John was losing his status and popularity. But to his credit, he did not feel threatened. John realized his purpose was not to establish himself but to prepare the way for another. His purpose was to recognize, raise up, and release the next leader who would bring the next great anointing.

In a very similar way, all leaders carry the mantle of John the Baptist. We all exist to prepare the way for another; to seek and search for the next one to lead, to raise him up, and release him into leadership. Even more, we should realize that part of that preparation is to accede some of our own status or importance in order to increase the status and importance of the one we are raising up.

Leaders must be willing to let go of control and give it to others. We must allow them to have authority and make decisions and enjoy the success and praise of those decisions. Kingdom leaders are not to grow in popularity and prestige like kings and heads of state, pulling more power and control to themselves. Instead, they should delegate and diminish. People should become less dependent on us and more dependent on those we are raising up. We should be decentralizing our power, decreasing our influence, and shifting it to others who will grow and learn from it and take it further.

In Mark 10, James and John had a worldly view of leadership. They believed it centered on personal power and having authority over others, even holding others down and using them to promote one's self. But Jesus rebuked that notion. He defined leadership as servanthood. Leaders in the Kingdom of God are great only when they serve the needs and interests of others rather than their own ambitions. This means when aspiring young Davids are coming up under us, we should not throw spears at them. Rather, we should "serve" them and their interests by encouraging and mentoring them.

Richard Langford wrote: *"There are two types of leaders: those who possess such an enormous presence in every aspect of their organization that the organization ceases to function when the leader is removed; and, effective ones. The good ones understand that leadership in the Kingdom of God is for the sake of the people. An organization that ceases to function when the leader is removed is one that essentially exists to sustain, serve, and glorify the leader and is therefore operating under a satanic model of leadership.*"[2]

Too many leaders today are trying to build an organization that is dependent on their own leadership. Rather than raising and empowering others to lead, they push them down, hinder their potential, and discourage them. This is not leadership, it's kingdom building. Leaders who do this are frauds. They are nothing more than dictators trying to establish a dynasty that perpetuates their own lust for power. Their goal is to grab more and more power and have more and more control. No one else can make decisions, initiate actions, or give commands. Everything must flow through them so they can retain their power and popularity. These are leaders after the order of Lucifer who wanted a throne to establish his glory.

By contrast, the great leaders are the ones who build an organization to last—more specifically, one that will outlast them. Great leaders are concerned, not about establishing themselves, but about establishing a lasting structure that sustains its values, fulfills its vision, and empowers its people independent of the leader's presence and control. They realize the need to widen the leadership base so the organization is not dependent on them, because they want the organization to survive and thrive when (not if) they are removed from leadership. They know that every leader will eventually abdicate his chair, but, rather than being gratified by the notion that people will suffer without them, they take steps to avoid such a dilemma because they truly put the people and the organization first. These are leaders after the order of Jesus Christ who built a church that would last because of the leaders He raised up and released with authority.

11 KEYS FOR RAISING LEADERS

Raising great leaders doesn't just happen. It happens because one is an intentional mentor. Our role as leaders is not just to promote a vision for an organization and manage its operations efficiently. Our role is also to raise up other potential leaders for that organization so its survival will surpass our own influence. The following are eleven disciplines that standing leaders must have to be great mentors of future leaders.

1. Be a Model of Great Leadership. Raising great leaders always begins with the character of the one who is doing the raising. If you are not a good example of leadership, then nothing else matters. First, be sure that when your followers look at you, they are seeing the qualities that they need to develop. Show them how important prayer is. Show them why it is essential to receive good counsel. Let them observe ethics in action. Be an example of hard work and humility. Explain to them why you do some of the things you do. Let your leadership become a classroom from which other aspiring leaders can learn.

2. Celebrate Their Unique Abilities. Recognize the special abilities or talents your protégé has and affirm them. Point them out in detail and compliment them. This will build their confidence and help them to realize that God has gifted them and called them to lead. When they accomplish some task or fulfill a role, be sure to praise them publicly and let others affirm them as well. Some leaders are unable to do this because they feel threatened or jealous. All this does is reveal how weak a leader they really are. The truly great leaders are constantly looking for ways to encourage, build, and edify those around them in hopes of propelling them forward in the calling God has for their lives.

3. Affirm Their Authority Publicly. Be sure to define their role as leaders to the entire organization. Everyone must know who this person is, what their title and job responsibility is, and that you have given them your full support. When people come to you with issues, challenges or complaints, be sure to direct them to your student which will reaffirm to all that you are serious about this person as a leader.

4. Give Them Opportunities to Shine. Some leaders are afraid to give their protégés responsibilities for fear that they will succeed. They are actually afraid that others will see that someone else can be equally important to the organization. They're afraid to lose their seat of preeminence. By contrast, we must give aspiring young leaders responsibilities, challenges, tasks, and duties that they will be able to, not only achieve, but achieve with great success. Then, once they succeed, we need to give them all the credit, acknowledge their accomplishment, and allow them to shine. Don't worry about it making them too proud. If they get proud, you'll deal with that. Instead see this as a way to build their confidence, promote assurance in their call, and push them forward.

5. Allow Them to Influence Your Decisions. One of the greatest ways to build leaders is to draw them into your inner circle and give them opportunities to speak into your vision. Not only does this build their worth and confidence, it teaches them how to develop and refine vision as well as how to be teachable (because you are being teachable). It also shows them how to process decisions and what to be sensitive to. It is an extremely important exercise in teaching young leaders how to make good decisions and avoid bad ones.

6. Allow Them to Make Their Own Decisions. Once you've delegated responsibilities to your protégé, let them lead. Don't try to micromanage them or second-guess their decisions. Let them make the call. You can help them recognize various dynamics and be sensitive to certain issues, but ultimately let them decide. And, more importantly, stand behind the decisions they make. Our followers will never learn to lead if they cannot be decisive. And the best place to learn decisiveness is under the watchful, supportive eye of a caring mentor.

7. Force Them to Live With Their Decisions. Of course, some of the decisions they will make will be bad ones. Rather than stepping in and fixing it for them, let them learn how to fix it themselves. As leaders, they're going to face conflicts, disagreements, and challenges. Many of those conflicts will come from their own actions or inactions and they are going to have to learn how to live with the consequences and make corrections where possible. Obviously, the astute leader will realize when intervention is needed and will step in. However, this is only a last resort after the student has learned how to tread water on his own for a while.

8. Provide Coaching and Encouragement. We must meet regularly with the people we are leading. Be sure to provide creative input and counsel. Always add a healthy dose of encouragement and "you can do it" affirmation. Most protégés will gain strength and confidence knowing that their leader is close by and always there to help if needed. Don't assume that everything is fine and that they don't need your input. They do. They're counting on it. Not necessarily to solve their problems, but to assure them that they're moving in the right direction.

9. Provide Accountability. If your student makes a mistake, be sure to hold them accountable. Explain what they did wrong and make sure they learned a lesson. Don't be afraid to hurt their feelings or discourage them. Leadership is often hard and full of discouragement. If they can't handle it, it's better to realize that now and find a new line of work.

10. Be Prepared to Be Less Popular Than Them. It's going to happen. Just accept it. If you raise up leaders, people will join their team, become loyal to them, and even like them more than you. Actually, that's a good thing. It means you're making them into good leaders that people want to follow. Don't try to hold onto popularity and feel important. Let others grow in their influence and become the leaders God has called them to be.

11. Be Prepared to Release Them and Let Them Go. It's hard because it means we're going to lose good people. It's troubling because they may even take others with them. It hurts because we love them and have poured so much into them. But the reality is: if you're a good leader and have done your job raising others to lead, you're going to have to say goodbye to people you love—a lot. You're going to have to let go and let God take them where He wants them to go. The good news is as you're faithful in raising up a few, God will give you more. It never fails. The more leaders I raise up and release, the more good people He adds to my team so I can train and raise them up as well. If you sow, you will reap. So be prepared to release them and let them Go!

A FINAL WORD

Finally, the greatest compliment to your leadership is the legacy of leaders that you have raised up to follow you. Do not limit the scope of your ministry by focusing only on the organization that is here and now. Have a long-term vision that transcends the present by raising up leaders whose influence will extend into the future. Sow into your church, ministry, or organization's tomorrow by raising up leaders today.

How The Mighty Have Fallen

Then Saul said to him, "Why have you conspired against me, you and the son of Jesse, in that you have given him bread and a sword, and have inquired of God for him, that he should rise against me, to lie in wait, as it is this day?" So Ahimelech answered the king and said, "And who among all your servants is as faithful as David, who is the king's son-in-law, who goes at your bidding, and is honorable in your house? Did I then begin to inquire of God for him? Far be it from me! Let not the king impute anything to his servant, or to any in the house of my father. For your servant knew nothing of all this, little or much." And the king said, "You shall surely die, Ahimelech, you and all your father's house!" Then the king said to the guards who stood about him, "Turn and kill the priests of the LORD, because their hand also is with David, and because they knew when he fled and did not tell it to me." But the servants of the king would not lift their hands to strike the priests of the LORD. And the king said to Doeg, "You turn and kill the priests!" So Doeg the Edomite turned and struck the priests, and killed on that day eighty-five men who wore a linen ephod. Also Nob, the city of the priests, he struck with the edge of the sword, both men and women, children and nursing infants, oxen and donkeys and sheep—with the edge of the sword.

1 Samuel 22:13-19

LESSON EIGHT

SAUL FAILED TO MANAGE CONFLICT

"Never is a leader's ability to lead more on trial than when confronted with conflict."

Gregg Johnson

Conflict is a fact of leadership. It is inevitable. And never is a leader's ability to lead more on trial than when confronted with conflict. It reveals a leader's steel. Either it will demonstrate his character and prove his credibility, or it will expose his deficiency and impotence to lead. Most people are impressed by a leader's number of followers or by the size of his or her organization. But, in truth, it is conflict that brings out the best or the worst, and reveals a leader's capacity to lead.

What began for King Saul as an opportunity with great promise soon became a nightmare of division, discord, and dissent. It began at the Valley of Elah where his failure to confront Goliath established David's legendary status in the eyes of all Israelites. The young lad with a stone and sling was hailed as a hero and Saul, who cowered in his tent, was mocked as David's inferior. The king knew that as long as

David lived, he could never be a leader in the hearts of the people.

From that time forward, enraged with jealously, Saul tried to hunt David down and kill him. It was a madness that thrust the nation into years of conflict. Anyone who was sympathetic toward David was branded an enemy of the state or even executed—as were Ahimelech, the priests, and the entire city of Nob. Rather than try to bring a resolution, restore relationships or reestablish peace and unity in the nation, Saul cared only about fortifying his position as king despite how it polarized the people. For Saul, his authority became a means to destroy anyone who disagreed or opposed him rather than trying to bring healing, strength, and peace back to the nation.

In essence, Saul was an abysmal failure at managing conflict. In fact, his leadership style and lust for power was the catalyst for conflict. Ironically, that which drove him to bolster his role as king ultimately led to his downfall and the eventual defeat of his regime. Such will be the outcome of any leader who fails to manage conflict and restore unity. Jesus said it like this: *"Every kingdom divided against itself is brought to desolation, and every city or house divided against itself will not stand"* (Matthew 12:25).

WHEN CONFLICT COMES

Ever since the early days of the church, there has been conflict. There was conflict when certain disciples thought their widows were being neglected (Acts 6:1). There was conflict over the import of Mosaic traditions in the church (Acts 15:2). When John Mark abandoned Paul and Barnabas in Pamphylia, it created conflict (Acts 15:37-39). The church at Rome had those who caused divisions and offenses (Romans 16:17). Even Jesus had to manage conflict between his own disciples (Mark 9:34).

"I hate confrontation," is the phrase we often hear from leaders but, unfortunately, conflict and confrontation cannot be avoided. If you are going to lead, you will encounter conflict. In fact, if you are not encountering conflict, you are probably not leading; more likely, you are just maintaining status quo. The question, therefore, for leaders, is not "how will you handle conflict 'if' it comes?" The question is "how will you handle conflict 'when' it comes?"

FIVE WAYS TO APPROACH CONFLICT

There are five typical approaches toward conflict. **The first is avoidance.** This is most common and occurs when the leader withdraws from conflict and avoids confrontation altogether. In an effort to justify his avoidance, he suppresses those who try to alert him of the issue and denies the conflict's very existence. This action (or inaction) will typically cause the conflict to resurface at some point in a more dramatic or adversarial form. Avoided conflict almost never goes away—like cancer that continues to grow unseen, its dangerous effects are simply postponed.[1]

Accommodation is the second approach to conflict. It reflects a high concern for preserving a relationship, even if it means surrendering one's own values. Using this approach is not necessarily resolving conflict; it is relinquishing ideals. It requires abandoning one's principles and convictions of right and wrong for fear of falling into disfavor with another. While this appears to be turning the other cheek, it actually leads to hidden anger and resentment, a lack of self respect, and even a sense of victimization.

The third attitude toward conflict is competition. This is characterized by a high concern for achieving personal goals even if it means offending or driving others away. The person who takes this approach will most likely be willing to sacrifice anything to achieve a personal goal—especially disrespecting people and sacrificing relationships.

Compromise is a fourth approach. King Solomon used this when two mothers argued over who owned a baby. He suggested a dramatic compromise: cut the child in half. Although effective in revealing the true mother, it shows us how ineffective compromise is in resolving conflict. Compromise occurs when both parties come to an agreement, but half-heartedly. They feel as though they have abandoned a principle or yielded some important value or moral for the sake of unity. People who feel they have compromised themselves have not truly resolved conflict; they have only repressed their convictions. Eventually they will grow to resent this and the conflict will resurface, or they abandon the cause altogether.

The fifth and most effective means of resolving conflict is collaboration. Collaboration occurs when both parties are more concerned about the health of the organization than they are about their own positions. Rather than compromising, each party works together to modify or delay their positions in a way that maintains their principles, but allows the other position to be observed as well. In the end, they are both focused more on the greater good of the body than they are about being right or getting their way.

This is, of course, the best way to resolve conflict. It allows each party to agree on a greater good and work together in achieving it. And, because they have worked together, they have "bought into" or "taken ownership" of the solution. So, the question is, "how do we facilitate a collaborative effort in resolving conflict in the church?"

PRACTICAL ISSUES IN MANAGING CONFLICT

Rehoboam the King was faced with a conflict in 1 Kings 12.

After his father Solomon died, the workers wanted to renegotiate their working conditions. Initially, it was an issue that could have been easily resolved. The offended parties were candid with their issues; they wanted to talk and welcomed the opportunity to reach a consensus. But how Rehoboam handled the issue caused it to escalate into a firestorm. Not only did the king not get his way, nine out of ten rejected his authority and rebelled against him.

Some leaders pride themselves in being confrontational. They pride themselves in tackling problems and putting things in order. However, we must be careful not to fall into the trap that snared Rehoboam. He was more concerned about being right than being in relationship. Rather than drawing people together and encouraging a collaborative resolution to conflict, he forced his agenda and drove people apart.

Obviously, there is a right way and a wrong to handle conflict. Although no set formula or procedure can resolve every disagreement, there are certain attitudes that can prevent them from escalating and may even encourage resolution. The key is relationship or being able to relate positively to one's counterpart. Those on opposite sides of conflict must be able to connect, communicate, and work together for the good of the organization.

A HEALTHY PERSPECTIVE

The first step in resolving conflict is having a proper perspective on the issue at hand. Rather than being concerned mainly about winning an argument, each party needs to focus on the bigger picture.

Redefine the conflict in terms of common ground. In other words, each side must come to a point of agreement concerning that "bigger picture." Establish what values are held in common and let that be the beginning point for discussion. For instance, the issue should not be identified as "one group wants blue carpet and the other wants green"; the issue is "we all want a church that shows excellence in appearance." Once a tenor for agreement has been set, other common values can be established such as "we all want to spend money wisely" or "we all want a carpet that will last for twenty years." Getting people to agree enables them to see each other as counterparts working for the same goal rather than opponents arguing a debate.

View the situation from your counterpart's perspective. This does not mean you have to agree with his or her perception of the situation, but you do need to understand what he or she feels is important, why he or she wants what he or she wants and why he or she is so opposed to your view. This will convey the idea that you truly care about your counterpart's concerns and respect his or her opinions. It has been said: "No one cares how much you know until they know how much you care." When they believe you care, they can begin to trust—which is essential in positive relationship—and the ability to work together.

Discuss each other's perceptions. Take time to "parrot" one another's responses. Say such things as, "So, what I'm hearing you say is..." or "Let me make sure I understand you..." and reframe your counterpart's statement in your own words. Such explicit discussion helps both sides to better understand each other while avoiding miscommunication. Also, such discussion may reveal common goals and strengthen the parties' relationship which leads to productive negotiations.

Propose solutions consistent with your counterpart's values. Having gained an understanding of the opposing viewpoint and what is important to them, focus on solutions that you know they would be amiable to. Everyone needs to feel the final resolution does not compromise their integrity.

Proposals which are consistent with your opponent's principles, and which do not undermine their self-image, are more likely to be accepted.

Allow for disagreement without being disagreeable. As discussion occurs, there will undoubtedly be objections to your opinions and rejections of your point of view. Expect this as a healthy part of conflict negotiation and avoid being insulted or defensive. Furthermore, when it is your turn to disagree, do it without being disagreeable. Be careful not to sneer, mock, roll your eyes or convey any kind of contempt. Maintain a posture of respectfulness and civility just as you would want others to do for you. Attitude is essential—which brings us to the next point.

A HEALTHY ATITTUDE TOWARD YOUR COUNTERPART

One of the surest ways to escalate conflict is to have a bad attitude about the other person. If you are serious about resolving conflict, then the first place to begin is with your own judgments about the opposition. You must make a decision to view your counterpart(s) as a person you must resolve things with and, therefore, must endeavor to have a positive attitude toward. The following are a few factors to keep in mind.

Be focused—on issues, not personalities. Many conflicts are exacerbated because one is offended or insulted by particular statements or people. As a result, they lose sight of the issue that needs to be resolved and focus on the person as an opponent to defeat. Try not to make it personal; don't see the conflict as a power struggle that you have to win in order to maintain your status or self respect. Again, you must never lose sight of the bigger picture.

Don't assume the worst about your opponent.

Suspicion means whatever your counterpart does, you will assume the worst about his motives. This makes it very difficult, if not impossible to work together. Moreover, if they discern such judgments from you, they will probably feel the same about you. However, if they sense you are giving them the benefit of the doubt, they will likely reciprocate. By the same token, if there has been a history of betrayal and broken promises impeding your ability to give one the benefit of the doubt, perhaps those issues need to be addressed first before any attempt at resolving the conflict occurs.

Avoid blaming your opponent for the problem. Blame, even if it is deserved, will only make your counterpart defensive. Even worse, your opponent may attack you in response. Blame is generally counterproductive.

Try to disprove your counterpart's worst beliefs and expectations about you. They may see you as proud, inflexible, and hard-headed. To make them receptive toward you, try to be disarming—do or say things that disprove your opponent's negative or inaccurate beliefs to help change those beliefs. Find things to genuinely compliment in your counterpart; this is not meant to patronize but to convey the message that you do respect the person and do not want to be adversarial.

Affirm the person's or group's worth to you. Reassure that they are valuable and appreciated by you. Show respect. Whether or not you always approve of other members' ideas, you should still be able to accept each other as valued members of the local body and the body of Christ.

Validate the other person's or group's offense. Don't be so focused on your own disappointment that you can't acknowledge how others have been hurt. Sometimes just acknowledging this breaks down barriers and opens the door to cooperation and collaboration

HEALTHY COMMUNICATION SKILLS

Negotiating conflict requires cool heads, calm emotions, and straightforward communication. Bad communication will cause discussions to deteriorate quickly and make matters worse. The following are a few examples of good communication skills.[2]

Prepare your mind in advance. Review your thoughts on issues you are going to discuss and edit them for accuracy. Mentally rehearse how you are going to present them. Try to anticipate the different objections you may encounter and how you would reasonably respond to them. Remember to be fair and reasonable in your approach.

Choose your words carefully. Words that are thoughtfully selected and respectfully expressed can provide direction and healing. But if words are carelessly or thoughtlessly used, spoken out of emotion or impulse, they can be incredibly hurtful and destructive.

Avoid provocative, accusatory language. Avoid statements that generalize and stereotype such as: "You always," "You never," "You can't," or "You won't." Such statements are unfair generalizations of a person's character and force people to become defensive and resistant.

Use more "I" statements than "You" statements. "I" statements tend to be informative: "I feel we should get started on...," or "I think it would be good for the church if we...." Whereas "You" statements tend to be accusatory: "You make me so angry," or "You always want the decisions to go your way." If you are offended and need to express anger, then own that anger and express it something like this: "When we talk about this subject, I tend to feel angry because...." This is much less accusing and inflammatory.

Don't interrupt. Let the other person finish what he or she is saying before you attempt to answer. That is very disrespectful and shows the person you have no interest in understanding him or her and have no respect for his or her ideas.

Become a good listener. Good listeners indicate they are hearing what is being said. They stop what they are doing; they don't doodle or skim through correspondence while someone else is speaking. They pay attention and indicate they are listening by facial expressions and appropriately responding with words or a nod of the head.

A HEALTHY DISPOSITION

Some people don't want to try to resolve conflict because they believe the other person simply has a bad attitude. They would rather allow things to deteriorate or escalate than put themselves in a situation where they believe they will be mishandled.

Be in control. Specifically, be in control of your emotions. Proverbs repeatedly reminds us of this: Proverbs 14:17, *"A quick-tempered man acts foolishly;"* Proverbs 14:29, *"He who is slow to wrath has great understanding, But he who is impulsive exalts folly;"* Proverbs 25:28, *"Whoever has no rule over his own spirit is like a city broken down, without walls."* Emotion always clouds one's judgment. Never react out of emotion. Avoid confronting someone when you are mad. Instead, give yourself some time to calm down. Remember, if you act out of emotion, you almost always have to apologize later.

Be reasonable. Convey a spirit of cooperation which sends the message "I want to work this out." There are times when ultimatums are appropriate: issues of immorality or doctrinal purity. These are not matters of conflict to be resolved, they are matters of biblical integrity that must be obeyed. However, be careful that philosophical or personal conflicts are not unduly escalated into unnecessary ultimatums. Be reasonable and willing to dialogue, negotiate and collaborate on a mutual solution.

Be humble. Many conflicts reach an impasse because of pride. Some believe their position, education, or title gives them the right to win. Humility is essential. Sincerely consider the other person's viewpoint and consider its legitimacy and potential for success. While it is important to explain why you have your particular point of view, don't be stubborn just because you want to win.

Be compassionate. Some conflicts escalate because the opposing parties are thinking mostly of winning and being right, but not about the bigger picture or the people being affected. True leaders must ask who is being negatively impacted by the conflict or how each person's proposed position will affect those who must abide by it.

Be flexible. Many conflicts are never resolved because people have invested so much in a position that they feel they must remain firm and loyal to it. Conflict can only be resolved when both parties are willing to negotiate. Is it really necessary to have things turn out just the way you want them? Or are there certain ideas or interests that you are willing to give up to end the conflict? What aspects are negotiable and non-negotiable; what are you willing to concede to?

While the above skills can be very helpful in resolving conflict, none of them can help without the central most important element: a healthy leader.

MANAGING CONFLICT REQUIRES A HEALTHY LEADER

If conflict can be resolved, it requires a healthy, sensitive, selfless leader: one who can set aside his own fears, insecurities and pride, and focus first on the needs and concerns of the people and the organization. This was the issue driving Israel's dilemma. That conflict was driven by one thing: an arrogant, headstrong, insensitive leader. Saul only cared about his perspective, his concerns, his needs, and his position. And it was this reckless abuse of authority that plummeted the nation into years of turmoil and decline.

Such is the case in many situations today. Often, it is an inept, insecure leader who cares only about "being right" and "looking good" that is fuelling conflict in an organization. Even conflicts not initiated by a leader can be exacerbated by him because of his own ego issues and fears of "losing face."

Jeremiah prophesied to the pastors who had become self-absorbed and insensitive to the condition of their people. He accused them of being dull-hearted and actually scattering the Lord's flock (Jeremiah 10:21; 23:2). Because they are so focused on their own needs and what makes them happy, they fail to attend to those issues that are dividing and scattering the sheep. This is important because the best way to manage conflict is proactively. It is to get out in front of the issue before it gains momentum and frame it in a healthy context. In order for a leader to do this he must be acutely tuned to the morale of the church rather than the morale of his ego.

TOXIC LEADERS CREATE CONFLICT

Ron Susek wrote: "No church is more than twenty-four hours away from a major conflict breaking out. In less than a year it can destroy years of hard work and growth."[3]

In other words, every church has within its ranks people who are volatile, contentious, and insubordinate. Every congregation contains people with attitudes and inclinations that have the potential to erupt into divisive, destructive forces. It is the disposition of the pastor that ultimately decides whether or not those rebellious spirits will rise to find a voice. His ability (or lack of ability) to relate to people, communicate effectively, and lead proactively determines if the culture of the church will promote dissention or encourage unity.

Plainly stated, leaders must set the tone for unity in the church by his or her own example. Sadly, some leaders have the kind of disposition and personality that seems to generate conflict and draw the worst out of people. They are contentious spirits or "toxic leaders." Proverbs 26:21 says, *"As charcoal is to burning coals, and wood to fire, so is a contentious man to kindle strife."* In 1 Timothy 6:4, Paul warns of those who are... *"Obsessed with disputes and arguments over words, from which come envy, strife, reviling (and) evil suspicions."* And, Proverbs 6:19 talks of he who *"...sows discord among brethren."* There are some people who seem to be magnets for conflict. Like an influenza patient spreading sickness wherever he goes, these people spread their disease as well. Wherever they go, there is an outbreak of conflict.

So what does a "Toxic Leader" look like? How can you tell if you are a leader with a contentious spirit?

First, a "Toxic Leader's" opinions are offensively absolute. He uses tones and makes statements that seem to suggest his way is the only way and anyone who disagrees is intellectually inferior. And if his idea is not accepted, he withholds his support from any other initiative and may even attempt to undermine it. On the contrary, healthy pastors who promote unity are willing to consider other opinions. They can receive criticism without becoming defensive and even support programs or initiatives that they may not be personally enthusiastic about but will participate in for the sake of supporting the people involved.

Second, a "Toxic Leader" sees only his own perspective. Because his opinions are absolute—or "from

God," there is no reason to try and understand any other person's perspective. They wrongly think: "These usurpers just need to submit." When others try to explain another perspective, they interrupt and talk over them; they don't even listen because they're only concerned about what they're going to say next. Healthy leaders however are skillful listeners. Romans 12:10 says *"in honor (they) give preference to one another."* They know that to build unity people must feel respected and valued; these leaders convey a sense of appreciation for the unique insights and perspectives that everyone brings to the table.

Third, the "Toxic Leader" uses a tone that is abrasive. His statements are often marked by harsh, inflammatory words and condemning tones. It is not what he says, but how he says it. Statements are made that are provocative—even offensive. If they disagree with someone (which is typical) their body language shouts rejection. They recoil and shake their head "disapprovingly." They roll their eyes, and cross their arms. Everything about them says, "No way!" Of course, it is not wrong to disagree, but skillful leaders—uniting leaders—are able to disagree without being disagreeable or communicating rejection. Unifying leaders value inclusion. They convey a sense of welcome and respect to everyone even if their ideas are dissimilar.

Fourth, the "Toxic Leader" would rather be right than be in a relationship. To this leader, winning an argument is more important than winning a soul (see Proverbs 11:30). Because he values his authority more than people and success as his greatest goal, those who disagree are seen as obstacles to overcome, rather than valued souls to "win over." But the wise leader knows how to "win souls." He knows when compromise is necessary; he understands that losing an argument can sometimes be a strategic step in winning a brother and, thereby, ultimately winning the war.

Fifth, "Toxic Leaders" are quick to criticize, correct and rebuke, but slow to encourage. In fact, rarely does a "Toxic Leader" offer any hint of encouragement. They see people as things to use to accomplish a goal. They are out of touch with what people feel and need. They care only that people do what they are told to do, the way they are told to do it; and if you do it wrong, beware the wrath of the contentious spirit. But good leaders are full of encouragement for those around them. In fact, when they offer correction, they are able to do so in a way that affirms people and inspires them to "want" to do better. They are not patronizing; they genuinely care about what people feel and need and believe their role as a leader is to help meet those needs.

Leaders who are humble and compassionate, leaders who convey a sense of worth and value to their followers, leaders who build a culture of inclusion where everyone matters and disagreement is met with respect are building a "Conflict Resistant Culture." Theirs will be an environment where mutual respect, acceptance, and seeking to understand one another will preclude the possibility of hostile disagreement. Just as a block of ice cannot remain long in a tropical environment, the frigid rigidity of conflict will melt under the warm spirit of compassion and genuine love.

MANAGING CONFLICT REQUIRES A HEALTHY CULTURE

Just as it is possible for the human body to build resistance against certain viruses and bacteria, it is also possible for certain organizations to become resistant toward conflict and division. It is something that must be woven into the culture or encoded in the DNA of the body.

Every leader must promote a "reconciling spirit" in his

congregation. Bill Hybels defines a reconciling spirit as an attitude that takes responsibility for resolving differences. It doesn't sit back and say, "It's not my fault. I am the one who has been hurt here. The other person is wrong and should come to me with an apology." Instead, the reconciling spirit takes the biblical high road of conflict resolution; it takes the initiative and says, "What can I do to resolve this conflict and be reconciled to my brother?" This means going directly to the person with whom one has a conflict—and with a humble spirit, expressing his or her commitment to walking in unity with the one who is offended.[4]

In addition to the presence of a reconciling spirit is the notion of "reverse accountability." If some offended individual is circulating a bad report in an effort to join others to their offense, these "others" will stop them mid-sentence and say, "I think you're talking to the wrong person. Please go to the individual with whom you're having this conflict and try to resolve it in a God-glorifying way." This is similar to what Jesus taught in Matthew 5 and Matthew 18.

How do leaders foster these dynamics in their congregations? There must be intentional teaching on themes such as love, humility, forgiveness and reconciliation. Jesus warned us that "offenses must come." The wise leader understands that on any given Sunday, there will be people in the pew who are carrying offenses—the seeds of conflict and division. Therefore, he will plan into his preaching schedule topical and expository sermons that deal with these issues directly and teach people how to resolve differences without bitterness or acting out. As well, when offended individuals come to church leaders with their complaints, rather than pamper and patronize them, the leaders should challenge them with the Word of God. They should be instructed according to Matthew 18 to go to that brother who sinned against them to seek resolution. Offended people should not be stroked, they should be firmly directed to resolve differences and then held accountable by the leader with whom they first expressed their offense.

A FINAL WORD

Conflict is a fact of leadership, but division does not have to be. It is the character and disposition of the leader that ultimately decides how conflict will spread or be resolved. Unfortunately, Saul was of such little character that he not only failed to resolve conflict, he perpetuated it. Effective leadership is by nature to manage and resolve conflict. Let us seek to rise above our own egos and need to be right and put the greater good of the organization first. Become a peacemaker and see how God will bless.

How The Mighty Have Fallen

Now Samuel had died, and all Israel had lamented for him and buried him in Ramah, in his own city. And Saul had put the mediums and the spiritists out of the land.

1 Samuel 28:3

Then Saul said to his servants, "Find me a woman who is a medium, that I may go to her and inquire of her." And his servants said to him, "In fact, there is a woman who is a medium at En Dor." So Saul disguised himself and put on other clothes, and he went, and two men with him; and they came to the woman by night. And he said, "Please conduct a séance for me, and bring up for me the one I shall name to you." Then the woman said to him, "Look, you know what Saul has done, how he has cut off the mediums and the spiritists from the land. Why then do you lay a snare for my life, to cause me to die?" And Saul swore to her by the LORD, saying, "As the LORD lives, no punishment shall come upon you for this thing."

1 Samuel 28:7-10

LESSON NINE

SAUL LACKED INTEGRITY

Most people have integrity until that integrity costs them something personally.

Gregg Johnson

King Saul had a problem with integrity. He was one thing publicly, but another thing privately. In public, he took a stand against mediums and drove them out of Israel, but in private, at least on one occasion, they were still a part of his life.

Integrity comes from the Latin word "integer" which means "one" or "wholeness." To have integrity means there is no double mindedness or duplicity in one's character. It is the condition of being whole—undivided in values and conduct. It is the struggle to be without contradiction in one's character.[1]

By contrast, Saul was duplicitous. He was double minded. He forbade others from seeking out witches and outlawed mediums from the land, but still harbored them in his own heart.

ABSOLUTES NEVER CHANGE

Absolutes are simply that, absolute. They are truths that

are not dependent on external conditions, opinions, or approvals for their nature or existence. They exist as sovereign realities simply because they are true. One plus one equals two is absolute. Two plus two equals four is absolute. These realities do not need personal interpretation or application to be true; they are correct on the basis of their own nature. Furthermore, by adhering to the principles of these mathematical realities, and many more like them, engineers have built bridges, put planes in flight, designed buildings that scrape the sky, and harnessed energy from nuclear fission.

In much the same way, the man of integrity recognizes certain moral absolutes and has integrated his life around them. Like the engineer adhering to principles of mathematics, the person of integrity commits to these absolutes as the guiding equations of his life. He believes them to be essential truths that will keep his home, his family, his ministry, his career, and all things secure. In fact, everything in his life depends on his recognizing and building his life upon those essential truths.

Integrity is the belief in certain absolutes and the commitment to integrate one's life around them. Jesus called it building on the rock. He likened His "sayings" to life principles—or absolutes—providing a firm foundation for our lives: *"Therefore whoever hears these sayings of Mine, and does them, I will liken him to a wise man who built his house on the rock: and the rain descended, the floods came, and the winds blew and beat on that house; and it did not fall, for it was founded on the rock. But everyone who hears these sayings of Mine, and does not do them, will be like a foolish man who built his house on the sand: and the rain descended, the floods came, and the winds blew and beat on that house; and it fell. And great was its fall"* (Matthew 7:24-27).

THE LIE OF MORAL RELATIVISM

Unfortunately, the notion of integrity, while celebrated in theory and respected in pretense, has been undermined by the popular philosophies of moral relativism.

Moral relativism is the belief that morality is relative. In other words there are no absolutes; there's no set of rules that applies to every person at all times regardless of situation or culture. It asserts that there can be no sovereign standard for deciding which of many opposing versions of right and wrong is correct or "true." In fact, the moral relativists will say each person is a sovereign being with his or her own understanding and interpretation of morality. Each person must decide "right from wrong" on his or her own. What's right for you may not be right for someone else. What's wrong for someone else may not be wrong for you. It's all relative to each person's own beliefs, cultural paradigms, and experiences. Essentially, moral relativism implies that 1 plus 1 may equal 2 for you; but for someone else it may equal 1.97. Furthermore, you have no right to impose your idea of "2" on someone else's idea of "1.97."

Of course, simple logic exposes the fallacy of this belief. By the standard of moral relativism, Martin Luther King Jr. had no right to impose his ideas of racial equality on the Ku Klux Klan who had different ideas concerning social justice. Similarly, terrorists who flew planes into buildings could not be judged as evil because, according to their personal convictions, they were acting righteously. For that matter, Hitler killing the Jews, Stalin exterminating Ukrainians, and Hutus murdering Tutsis did nothing "wrong." They were simply correcting their perspectives of centuries of injustice and societal waste. At least that's what moral relativism would say.

Obviously, the average person is not so extreme in their philosophical persuasions. Most people practice their brand of moral relativism by using the simple phrase, "That depends." You may ask, is lying wrong? They'll say, "That depends. If lying will get me a promotion and provide more money for my family, then lying is good." Is stealing wrong? Again the relativist would say, "That depends. If stealing something can improve my living standard (and no one gets hurt), then lying isn't wrong." Is it bad to leave your spouse? "That depends. Doesn't God want me to be happy? And if I find someone who makes me happy, isn't that good?" Take that reasoning to the extreme and it's no different than a KKK member justifying his hatred of minorities or the terrorist strapping explosives to his vest. Right and wrong are decided, not by an independent code of absolutes, but by my own perspectives and personal preferences.

This is what Jesus referred to as building on the sand.

INTEGRITY ARISES FROM PRINCIPLES

The person of integrity is a person of principle. They are guided by absolutes: an internalized set of rules that guides their decisions and determines their course of conduct. They are firm on what is right and what is wrong. Of course, they are not perfect and may fall short of their convictions from time to time. But, at the core, they struggle to remain consistent with the values in which they believe.

For the Christian, this matter is clear cut. Our standard is God's Word, the Bible. Scripture is the standard, the authoritative rule for faith and conduct in this life. Beginning with the Ten Commandments and extending through the Epistles of Paul, these truths provide foundational principles that serve as the basis for integrity.

Unfortunately, living in a culture of moral relativism means that right and wrong will not always be easily defined. Not every issue can be connected to a Bible reference. There will often be matters of conscience or grey areas in which the person of integrity must apply the spirit of certain principles to the issues before them. It is in these instances that outcomes and consequences apply. In other words, how will this decision affect me, those around me, and my relationship with God?

The following are five questions any man or woman of integrity needs to ask when contemplating such matters of conscience.

Does it contradict God's Word? This is an obvious question to ask, but it does not go without stating. 2 Timothy 3:16 states: *"All Scripture is given by inspiration of God, and is profitable for doctrine, for reproof, for correction, for instruction in righteousness."* First and foremost, is there any scripture, value or implied principle that addresses the issue I am contemplating? Is it prohibited, condemned or in any way discouraged? If so, the choice is clear: abstain.

Does it feed my flesh? In 1 Corinthians 6:12, Paul wrote, *"All things are lawful for me, but all things are not helpful."* In 1 Corinthians 10:23 he wrote, *"All things are lawful...but not all things edify."* Paul was saying, just because there may not be a scripture or a command to prohibit certain things does not mean I should feel free to do those things. The issue is not whether the activity is outlawed in scripture, the issue is whether doing this thing will build me up spiritually (will it benefit or edify me) or will it drag me down and hinder me spiritually?

To this point, Galatians 5:16-17 says, *"Walk in the Spirit, and you shall not fulfill the lust of the flesh. For the flesh lusts against the Spirit, and the Spirit against the flesh; and these are contrary to one another, so that you do not do the things that you wish."* Romans 13:14 tells us to *"Put on the Lord Jesus Christ, and make no provision for the flesh, to fulfill its lusts."* As disciples of Christ we should not be trying to live as close to the world and sin as possible without losing our salvation. Our desire should be to place things in our lives that strengthen our walk with God and avoid those things that do not. Should I go to that movie? Should I attend that reception? Should I take that job? There may not be a clear command in scripture to direct you, but your decision should be clearly based on whether or not that activity will feed your flesh or fill your spirit.

Does it tarnish my testimony? 1 Peter 2:12 tells us to *"have your conduct honorable among the Gentiles, that when they speak against you as evildoers, they may, by your good works which they observe, glorify God in the day of visitation."* As witnesses for Christ, we are expected to be a force for good in this world. Lost people should look at our lives and not only see a reflection of Jesus Christ, but the positive difference God's redeeming grace has made in us. Compromises in our testimony undermine this possibility. It gives people cause to question the validity of our faith and the authenticity of God's redeeming power in our lives. The next time you attend a worldly event that promotes immorality or have the opportunity to be among unsaved people while they celebrate carnality, ask yourself whether this is a positive reflection on your witness for Jesus, or whether it is inconsistent with Christ's character and runs contrary to integrity.

Does it offend my authorities? God has provided spiritual authorities for three reasons: guidance, protection, and accountability. Our leaders are not there to control us; they are there to help us see things that we could not otherwise recognize on our own. Hebrews 13:17 says, *"Obey those who rule over you, and be submissive, for they watch out for your souls, as those who must give account. Let them do so with joy and not with grief, for that would be unprofitable for you."* If you have an unsettled feeling regarding a decision, talk to your leader about it. Get his or her feedback. God has placed him or her in your life to help you and watch out for your souls. However, be ready to accept the fact that your leader may actually confirm the check you are having in your spirit about some activity and be willing to submit to his or her counsel.

Does it stumble my followers? 1 Corinthians 8:9, 12-13 says, *"Beware lest somehow this liberty of yours become a stumbling block to those who are weak. ...But when you thus sin against the brethren, and wound their weak conscience, you sin against Christ. Therefore, if food makes my brother stumble, I will never again eat meat, lest I make my brother stumble."* Here Paul is stating to the Corinthians that although we may be free from keeping the law, we still have a solemn responsibility to other believers, especially new Christians who can easily be confused or discouraged by the freedom we feel to participate in questionable activities.

This is an especially important issue for leaders because people are looking to us as examples. Like it or not, we are producing disciples who will model their behaviors and personal standards after our own. We must be careful that those things we feel free to participate in (such as drinking alcohol, participating in questionable entertainment, or attending world activities) could actually cause our followers to lower their own personal standards and become drawn into carnal activities while convincing themselves it is acceptable because "my leader does it."

INTEGRITY REQUIRES COURAGE

Most people have integrity until that integrity costs them something personally. It's our willingness to pay a price for our morals that demonstrates if the integrity we claim to have is real or mere pretense. True integrity is holding to principles regardless of personal cost. Make no mistake, integrity has a price and if you want to be known as a person of integrity, there will be a cost involved.

It was easy for Daniel (in Daniel 1:8) to abstain from pagan foods while living in Jerusalem where pagan food was taboo. It was easy for him to maintain a strict diet when everyone else was keeping the same diet. The real test of integrity came in Babylon, when he was expected—even commanded—to eat pagan foods. It was when his principles required him to defy the king, take a stand and say, "No. I won't!" It was when there was a potential cost involved that his integrity was authentically demonstrated.

I was easy for Shadrach, Meshach, and Abed-Nego (in Daniel 3:13-18) to refuse to bow before idols in Israel where idolatry was frowned upon. That's not showing integrity. True integrity was shown when Nebuchadnezzar commanded them to bow under threat of execution if they refused. True integrity was revealed when the guards heated the furnace, bound them with chains and still they refused to bow. True integrity was shown when they were tossed into the fire and would not betray their convictions even expecting death to ensue. That is integrity, when it costs.

Paul confronted Peter in Galatians 2:11-14 because he wasn't willing to pay the price of integrity. Rather than be a consistent disciple of Christ and accepting Gentiles without circumcision, Peter withdrew from them and preferred company with the Jews fearing their rejection. Paul told him he was guilty of compromise and betrayed the principles of the gospel because he lacked the courage to bear integrity's cost.

True integrity will be tested. It has a price which can only be paid by the courageous—the one who is willing to lose friends, become unpopular, face rejection, mockery, insult and even injury. Integrity costs.

Have you ever had to pay for your integrity? What did it cost you? It cost a stockbroker his job when he refused to withhold negative figures from quarterly reports. It cost a young carpenter his apprenticeship when he refused to build a bar that would serve alcohol to alcoholics. It cost a teenager his popularity when he continued to publicly confess Christ as his Lord and Savior.

Unfortunately, most people do not do what is "right," they do what is "right for me." They do what is morally convenient and serves their interests for the moment. "If telling the truth makes me look good, I'll tell the truth. If it makes me look bad, I'll lie." Or, "If being honest helps me advance my career, I'll be honest. But if exaggerating the facts gives me a boost, I'll exaggerate." Or, "If being married makes me happy, I'll stay with my wife. If not, I'll leave her for some other woman."

But the person of integrity will tell the truth regardless of how embarrassing the truth may be. He will be faithful to his marriage regardless how much sacrifice is required to save it. He will reject sinful activity regardless of who it may offend or how unpopular he may become.

Integrity costs. Integrity requires courage.

INTEGRITY IS WHAT HAPPENS IN PRIVATE

Integrity means doing what is right when no one is watching. Psalms 101:2 says, *"I will walk within my house with a perfect heart."* The old saying is still true: "Integrity is when you do the right thing even though no one is watching." It's what we do when we're all alone, when no one is there to appreciate our goodness or rebuke our badness that defines the authenticity of our integrity. Anyone can stand in the pulpit and declare high ideals to the admiration of the crowd. As well, anyone can avoid doing wrong when he knows he's being monitored in the spotlight. It's what a man will do when he knows he will get away with it that reveals how much integrity he really has.

Every second, over twenty-eight thousand internet users are viewing pornography. Every thirty-nine minutes, a new porn video is being uploaded to an industry that makes over three million dollars every second.[2] A survey by *Leadership Magazine* showed 40 percent of pastors regularly struggle with pornography.[3]

These trends reveal that a large number of Christian leaders have an integrity issue. In the pulpit or in the boardroom they may champion the standards of biblical holiness, but in private they are something completely different. There is a double-mindedness; a duplicity of character. And leaders need to beware; these little compromises are the cracks in our defense through which the enemy comes in like a flood.

A remark was made concerning a minister who "fell" into adultery. However, no one simply "falls into sin." Falling into sin is a process of consistently giving into temptation—especially secret temptation. James 1:14-15 says, *"...each one is tempted when he is drawn away by his own desires and enticed. Then, when desire has conceived, it gives birth to sin; and sin, when it is full-grown, brings forth death."* Falling into sin is the progressive descent of one's moral integrity. Hebrews 2:1 calls it "drifting." The scripture says, *"We must give the more earnest heed to the things we have heard, lest we drift away."* The picture is given of a boat with a sailor. Instead of the sailor rowing hard and intently toward safe harbor, the vessel gets caught in the currents and tides swirling about it and is pulled out to sea and lost. In order for a boat not to drift, there must be something in that boat that has more power to drive it than does the current to drift it. That's what integrity is; it's that inner engine, our principles and convictions that drive us against those currents threatening to pull us out to sea.

But drifting occurs when we give liberties where none should be given. We make allowances and tolerate compromises instead of maintaining personal standards—especially in private. Eventually, we become accustomed to living below the line of moral integrity; what were once considered moral felonies have been reduced (in our minds) to moral misdemeanors.

Such was the case with Samson—a man anointed with great strength. He permitted his flesh to go beyond the boundaries prescribed by God. He saw what he shouldn't have seen, went where he shouldn't have gone, and ended up doing what he shouldn't have done. It all started with little compromises and the lowering of personal standards. All the while, Samson convinced himself that he was okay. He seemed to still have an anointing. He still had his strength. He could still overpower the Philistines, tear down gates and break the ropes Delilah wrapped around his wrists. God appeared to be with him. However, the time eventually came when "he didn't realize the Spirit of the Lord had left him."

It's the "Samson Syndrome" and so many are ensnared by it today. Many leaders are "seeing what they shouldn't see, going where they shouldn't go, and doing what they shouldn't do." Sadly, they've convinced themselves they are okay: "I still feel God's presence in worship. I still preach the Word with unction. I still have His anointing when I pray for the sick. God is with me, this little compromise isn't affecting me." But what they don't realize is that the Holy Spirit is being grieved. Eventually he will be quenched and, regretfully, if compromise continues, His anointing will depart.

Integrity is not true unless it passes the privacy test. True integrity is what happens when no one is watching and I know I can get away with compromising it. If you want to be anointed in public, learn first how to be anointed in private. Learn how to honor God, walk in purity, and maintain integrity in secret and God will bless you openly.

INTEGRITY TELLS THE TRUTH

Recently, a renowned songwriter inspired millions of believers with a worship song he wrote based on his "battle" with terminal cancer. The song, aptly called "Healer," rose quickly to number two on Australia's official music charts and soon after became a global phenomenon driven by the dramatic testimony of this courageous young songwriter. That is, until the songwriter was discovered to be a fraud that had never been diagnosed with cancer. He confessed to have "made up" the story to get more publicity and recognition for his "worship song."

Proverbs 12:22 says, *"Lying lips are an abomination to the Lord, but those who deal truthfully are His delight."* Ephesians 4:25 says: *"(put) away lying, let each one of you speak truth with his neighbor."* By contrast, studies reveal that 91 percent of people lie regularly, 69 percent admit to frequently lying to their spouses, and 32 percent believe that they've been lied to by their pastor. Further, Paul Elkman, in his book, *Telling Lies*, claims that the average ten-minute conversation contains approximately three lies.

So what is "lying?" That's easy one may say: "It's a statement that misleads or deceives someone." But lying is more than a deceptive statement—lying is any action or intention that misleads, deceives, or misrepresents the truth.

What is more, lying is not just done with words. One can lie without even speaking or by revealing only so much of the truth that it leads someone to believe the wrong thing. For instance, a pastor says, "We had fifty new people join the church this year." Obviously, this leads you to believe that he has fifty more people in his church this year than he did last year. But, what he didn't tell you was that last year, sixty people left his church, so he actually has ten less.

What is "Biblical Honesty?" 1 Peter 2:1 says, *"Therefore, lay aside all guile (or deceit)."* Honesty, as the Bible defines it, means avoiding statements or actions (such as giving partial information, or making out-of-context statements, or even maintaining silence) that are intended to create beliefs or leave impressions that are untrue or misleading. This level of honesty even implies volunteering information another person needs to know to achieve an accurate understanding of the truth. Michael Josephson, founder of the Josephson Institute of Ethics states, "Honesty is a good-faith intent to convey the truth as best we know it and to avoid communicating in a way likely to mislead or deceive."[4]

When it comes to integrity, there is no greater demonstration than that of integrity. People who are found to be deceptive or misleading are immediately deemed untrustworthy, lacking in credibility, and are dismissed out of hand. To be regarded as a person of integrity, one must zealously guard his reputation for honesty. This means more than merely speaking truthful facts; it is being truthful in nature. It goes to motives and intention. It holds the standard of bringing others into an accurate and straightforward understanding of the truth as it is known to be without any motive to mislead or misinform.

INTEGRITY KEEPS ITS WORD

Psalm 15:1-4 tells us, *"Who may abide in Your tabernacle? Who may dwell in Your holy hill? He who walks uprightly...He who swears to his own hurt and does not change."* James 5:12 says it like this, *"...let your 'Yes,' be 'Yes,' and your 'No,' 'No,' lest you fall into judgment."* Too often people who lack integrity say "yes" but then their "yes" quickly changes to "no."

It is important to understand that the ethic of keeping one's word is an absolute. It is a universal principle, revealed in God's Word, intended for all who would "abide in His tabernacle" to observe. Unfortunately, I have seen in some cultures where "keeping your word" doesn't matter or hold much value.

There are those who are quick to say "yes" or agree to something because they don't want to be impolite or seem disrespectful to the authority who is asking them. To say "no," they reason would be too bold, too defiant and disrespectful. So they agree, in the moment, mostly because they want to be polite, not necessarily because they intend to follow through. When the time comes for the job to be done or the thing to which they agreed to be performed, they easily disregard the promise they made. It's easy because, in their mind, it was more important to be polite than it was to do the thing they agreed to do. What they fail to realize is that it is a greater act of disrespect to say yes and then not do it. It is far more impolite to leave your friend stranded, fail to provide the assistance needed, or let the leader down who was counting on you. Not only have you disrespected your friend, you have disrespected yourself by devaluing your character, integrity, and your credibility.

This is also true in the church by well-meaning members. People are often stirred by their emotions to commit to some worthy cause only to fall away when the duty becomes laborious, tiring, or just plain boring. According to James 1 such people are "double minded" and unstable in all of their ways. Conversely, integrity means oneness or wholeness. It means there is no double mindedness or duplicity in a person's character. In other words, they can be counted on to follow through on what they said they would do.

Robert Service said, "A promise made is a debt unpaid." The man of integrity takes his word very seriously. Anytime he gives his word, makes a promise or commits, it is (to him) like incurring a debt: a debt that can only be satisfied by doing what's been promised.

What ever happened to these simple concepts: keeping our word or making a promise and fulfilling it? For this, there can be no substitute. It is sad to encounter leaders who lack integrity in such little things as keeping an appointment, being on time, or following through on a commitment. If you can't do that, scripture says you're double minded, unstable, and have the character of a false prophet. Deuteronomy 18:22 tells us that if a prophet's words do not come to pass, he should be rejected as a fraud. Men of God who give their word but fail to fulfill it should be esteemed no better.

INTEGRITY BRINGS SECURITY

In ancient China, the people desired security from the barbaric hordes to the north, so they built "The Great Wall of China." It was so high they knew no one could climb over it and so thick that nothing could break it down. So, they settled back to enjoy their security. During the first hundred years of the wall's existence, however, China was invaded three times. Interestingly, not once did the barbaric hordes break down the wall or climb over the top. History tells us that, each time, they bribed a gatekeeper who opened the doors and allowed them to march right through the gates. The Chinese were so busy relying upon the great walls of stone that they neglected to find gatekeepers who were men of integrity.

Proverbs 10:9 tells us, *"He who walks with integrity walks securely, but he who perverts his ways will become known."* One's life may be filled with great accomplishments, but it is integrity that keeps those accomplishments secure. One may have a successful career and draw the admiration of great men; but it is integrity that will keep that success secure. One may have been blessed with a wonderful wife and a healthy marriage; but it is integrity that will keep that marriage secure. One may be a leader in the Kingdom of God whose ministry is flourishing and, like the Great Wall of China, it seems to have been built high and strong, and able to withstand any attack. But, where integrity is lacking there are open doors for the enemy to gain entrance and bring destruction.

Richard Dresselhaus wrote, *"Rarely does a pastor fail because he is a poor preacher, inadequately trained, or unsure of his call. Typically, pastors fail over matters that have to do with character. They compromise in the little and hidden things that over time undermine the integrity of their ministry and render their service for God ineffective."*

Saul was a leader who lacked integrity and it became his downfall. God had promoted him to the pinnacle of success but his character was unable to support it. Are we men and women of integrity? Success and promotion will bring many temptations and opportunities to compromise our morals. But the leaders that have integrity will stand. Integrity keeps us consistent, reliable, and honest: qualities which provide a foundation to support a leader's enlargement.

How The Mighty Have Fallen

How The Mighty Have Fallen

Now the Philistines fought against Israel; and the men of Israel fled from before the Philistines, and fell slain on Mount Gilboa. Then the Philistines followed hard after Saul and his sons. And the Philistines killed Jonathan, Abinadab, and Malchishua, Saul's sons. The battle became fierce against Saul. The archers hit him, and he was severely wounded by the archers. Then Saul said to his armorbearer, "Draw your sword, and thrust me through with it, lest these uncircumcised men come and thrust me through and abuse me." But his armorbearer would not, for he was greatly afraid. Therefore Saul took a sword and fell on it. And when his armorbearer saw that Saul was dead, he also fell on his sword, and died with him. So Saul, his three sons, his armorbearer, and all his men died together that same day.

1 Samuel 31:1-6

LESSON TEN

SAUL DESTROYED HIMSELF

Leadership will destroy the man whose character has not been prepared for it.

Gregg Johnson

Saul killed himself. Overrun by the enemy, his army crushed, and mortally wounded by arrows, Saul took a sword and fell on it. Indeed, the enemy had overpowered him, but in the end his death was his own doing.

It was a tragic end that serves as a metaphor for all leaders. We must take heed lest our success be our undoing. The saying is true: "With higher levels come higher devils." Leadership will destroy the man (or woman) whose character has not been prepared for it. With advancement, promotion and enlargement in the Kingdom of God comes fiercer attacks, harsher resistance, and more intense warfare. The battle gets tougher the higher you go; and leaders must be aware that in the midst of such intense warfare there is a danger to fall on their own swords.

Proverbs 5:22-23 reinforces this concern by warning: *"His own iniquities entrap the wicked man, and he is caught in the cords of his sin. He shall die for lack of instruction, and in the greatness of his folly he shall go astray."* The warning is clear: men are often ensnared by *their own iniquities* and *the greatness of their own folly*. In other words, our concern should not just be for the traps the devil is setting for us and the arrows he is shooting; we should be equally concerned about the traps we are setting for ourselves. We leaders need to be careful lest we fall on our swords in battle.

The context of Proverbs 5 gives us great insight into the number one cause of so many fallen leaders: sexual sin. Proverbs 5:20 plainly says, *"Why should you, my son, be enraptured by an immoral woman, and be embraced in the arms of a seductress?"* It is an issue as old as leadership itself: the most common way that leaders self-destruct is sexual sin. More and more we hear about good men who have committed adultery or partake in pornography and are falling on their swords. It's not only the arrows of the Philistines killing them, they're killing themselves. Good men fall into sexual immorality, not because of the devil's traps but because of the traps they have set for themselves. The paths they travel, the practices and policies they have, instead of keeping them safe, expose them to dangers, snares, and falling on swords.

A survey by *Leadership Magazine* showed 40 percent of pastors regularly struggle with pornography.[1] Other research reveals that 37 percent of pastors have been involved in inappropriate sexual behavior with someone in their church.[2] Even more alarming is a 15-year study that revealed approximately 10 to 12 percent of ministers have engaged in sexual intercourse with members of their congregations.[3] Sadly, these statistics indicate a growing promiscuity in ministry that is reflective of our culture. Wayne Goodall, in his book, *Why Great Men Fall,* revealed that 25 percent of wives and 44 percent of husbands have had extramarital intercourse.

As is true with church leaders, many of their affairs began at "work." Fifty percent of unfaithful wives were involved with someone from work and 62 percent of unfaithful men likewise met their affair partners at work.[4] Indeed sexual promiscuity is occurring in epidemic proportions in our day.

So as we see Saul slumped over on the battlefield, a sword sticking into his chest, we should be concerned, not only about the arrows the enemy shoots at us, but about the traps we set for ourselves. It is not Satan who is causing pastors to fall into adulterous affairs; pastors fall because of their own folly. They fall because of careless professional ethics and negligent standards of personal purity.

Throughout scripture we see examples of leaders who battled the arrows of sexual temptation. Some overcame victoriously, others self-destructed. The following is a survey of some of these men and women and lessons they teach us.

JOSEPH AND POTIPHAR'S WIFE
RUN FROM DANGER

"And it came to pass after these things that his master's wife cast longing eyes on Joseph, and she said, 'Lie with me.' But he refused ...So it was, as she spoke to Joseph day by day, that he did not heed her, to lie with her or to be with her. But it happened about this time, when Joseph went into the house to do his work, and none of the men of the house was inside, that she caught him by his garment, saying, 'Lie with me.' But he left his garment in her hand, and fled and ran outside" (Genesis 39:7-12).

Scripture describes Joseph as a handsome man to whom Potiphar's wife was attracted. It is a reminder that leadership is attractive. There will always be those, especially of the opposite sex, who admire the one who leads. Leadership makes a person more appealing. It provides an image of charisma, confidence, and decisiveness. Often the more ignoble aspects of a person, their lesser qualities are obscured by the spotlight and people are easily enamored by the image they see in the pulpit.

Wise leaders, however, will realize the snare of the spotlight, and will employ measures to deliver them from sexual sin. Like Joseph, they will run; they will avoid those situations that will ensnare and cause them to fall on their sword.

Avoid being alone with the opposite sex. Joseph got into trouble because he was alone with another man's wife, even though his intentions were innocent. Romans 13:14 instructs us to *"Make no provision for the flesh, to fulfill its lusts."* 1 Thessalonians 5:22 further warns us to *"Avoid every appearance of evil."* This means that leaders must demonstrate due diligence in avoiding situations that present temptation or have the appearance of impropriety, even if intentions are innocent.

Foremost is the danger of being alone with the opposite sex. In a car, having a meeting, sharing a lunch, holding a counseling session—it may seem innocent to you but it has the potential of sending the wrong signal. It says, "I'm interested in you, I don't mind being alone with you," or even worse, "I enjoy being alone with you."

Furthermore, having "alone time" with the opposite sex causes others to question your integrity. If someone sees you alone with that person in a restaurant, in a car, or behind closed doors, more than likely, they will be suspicious and inherently sense something inappropriate. This means men who are spiritual leaders should not have private prayer meetings with women. They shouldn't have one-on-one counseling sessions with women or drive in the car alone with them and never, never, never have lunch or dinner alone with the opposite sex—even in a crowded restaurant.

If I must meet with the opposite sex—I will not meet in a place where we are alone. I always try to meet with others present in the room. If that is not possible or practical, then I will always leave the door open or at least ajar. This sends the message, "We are not really alone" or "I am uncomfortable being alone with you" or more importantly, "I don't want to be alone with you."

In fact, I have instructed my staff on several occasions, "Never leave me alone in the building when there is a woman in my office." And "If you see me in my office with a woman, never pull the door shut, always leave it ajar." As a result, on more than one occasion, someone on my staff has remained late in the office so as to avoid leaving me in a compromising situation.

Another solution may be to install a window in your office or to replace your door with one that has a widow in it. Of course, be sure that curtains or blinds are not covering these windows when counseling someone.

Some may feel these measures are too extreme or somewhat paranoid. However, I don't believe one can be too careful in the area of sexual purity. I have served three pastors in my over twenty-four years of ministry. Of those three men, two of them have fallen prey to adultery, have divorced their wives and been removed from pastoral ministry. I have personally witnessed how a casual, relaxed attitude toward the opposite sex can expose good men to subtle and destructive snares.

Avoid excessive physical contact with opposite-sex parishioners. In the book, *Does Touching Patients Lead to Sexual Intercourse?*, published research reveals that physical exchanges such as hugs, touches, pats, and putting one's arms around the shoulders correlates to a high risk for later sexual encounters.[5] The studies also reveal that such contact is not as innocent or indiscriminate as one may insist, but is often directed toward those that one is physically attracted to.

Some pastors say, "I just love everybody and want to give everyone a big hug." That may sound fatherly and pastoral—but it is also naive and foolish. These leaders are ignoring the fact that many people have been impaired by a sexually obsessed culture and could be confused by our good intentions. In fact, those who have suffered sexual mistreatment often cannot distinguish between erotic and non-erotic hugs and any touch at all might cause them fear, pain, sexual arousal, and flashbacks.[6]

Add to this the reality that such physical contact often awakens the leader to temptation, especially when physical attraction exists. A recent *Leadership* survey of nearly a thousand pastors revealed that 12 percent admitted to extramarital intercourse. Among those with whom pastors were involved sexually, 69 percent came from within their own congregations, including 17 percent who were in a counseling relationship with the pastor. The primary reason for the sexual encounter was physical and emotional attraction as noted by 78 percent of the pastors, while marital dissatisfaction was reasoned by 41 percent.[7] Clearly, ministers and church leaders who are physically attracted to the opposite sex are vulnerable to sexual temptation and it would be wise not to exacerbate it with unnecessary physical contact.

This is not to say that any physical contact is always wrong. There may be times when one is reunited with old friends or when special events engender a congratulatory hug. However, these kinds of exchanges should be the exception, not the norm. Leaders who wish to express affection through frequent use of hugs, kisses, and tight embraces should reserve them for his or her own spouse. Giving regular physical affection to others of the opposite sex is simply inappropriate.

Avoid discussing inappropriate issues with the opposite sex. Spiritual leaders must use extreme caution when discussing sexual issues, especially with a person of the opposite sex. Dr. Wayne Goodall makes this point when he writes, *"Do you share about your own sex life? Do you initiate conversation about sexual problems, preferences, or fantasies for the purposes of sexual gratification? Do you make comments on sexual or physical characteristics or imagined sexual performance? Counselor licensing boards consider this sexual exploitation, and it may be punishable as a felony criminal offense."*[8]

Such discussions are dangerous because they cross thresholds that should be reserved for counselors of the same sex—or husbands and their wives. When church leaders broach these subjects with the opposite sex, it connects them on an emotionally intimate level. Even worse, sensual ties will develop that leave both parties open to temptation. Sometimes, that temptation is too great when one or both of those parties are in an emotionally weakened condition, lonely, in need of affirmation, or physically attracted to one another.

Never take advantage of the power differential you hold over a parishioner. People often put their pastors on pedestals. They give spiritual leaders a great deal of trust while affording them unusual access to and influence over their lives. Sadly, some leaders have leveraged this authority to gratify their own needs.

I received a phone call from one unfortunate woman who was disturbed about a pastor who told her she needed "deliverance." He used his "spiritual expertise" to diagnose her condition, invite himself into her home—alone—and conduct numerous exorcisms. The woman was troubled, not only by this pastor's diagnosis of her spiritual condition, but the "techniques" used to deliver her. They involved placing his hands on her and pressing his body against hers in a very intimate way. This pastor was taking advantage of his spiritual clout and the trust this woman had placed in him to gratify his own urges.

"How terrible!" one might exclaim. Indeed. Yet how often are these scenarios replayed in churches today—but with less extreme methods? What about church leaders who offer friendly hugs and kisses to the young, attractive ladies in the church? Or the deacon who meets privately to console the distressed divorcee? And then there is the elder who takes advantage of those he knows are needy and emotionally weakened, to flirt with them or gratify himself in some way emotionally or physically. Unfortunately, it happens all too often.

Dr. Gary Collins, in his book, *Excellence and Ethics in Counseling*, indicates that so many people have been emotionally damaged by the sexual advances of counselors, ministers, and those in authority over them that Masters and Johnson asserted such behavior should be labeled and prosecuted as a form of rape.[9] The presence of so many men holding positions of authority over women—especially in the church—obligates these men to be especially cautious and discreet when dealing with women. Even if some of these leaders are unpaid volunteers, they are in authority and leverage a certain amount of power. They must apply the same standards of professionalism and restraint as do the pastors who are being paid to act professionally.

SAMSON AND DELILAH
AVOID EMOTIONAL ATTACHMENTS

"Afterward it happened that he loved a woman in the Valley of Sorek, whose name was Delilah. And the lords of the Philistines came up to her and said to her, 'Entice him, and find out where his great strength lies, and by what means we may overpower him, that we may bind him to afflict him; and every one of us will give you eleven hundred pieces of silver.' So Delilah said to Samson, 'Please tell me where your great strength lies, and with what you may be bound to afflict you.' Then she lulled him to sleep on her knees, and called for a man and had him shave off the seven locks of his head. Then she began to torment him, and his strength left him" (Judges 16:4-6, 19).

Samson fell in love with a woman he had no business being in love with. He became emotionally attached to a Philistine, the same enemies of Israel that defeated King Saul. In much the same way, leaders today are allowing themselves to become emotionally attached to women they have no business being attached to and setting a snare for themselves.

Leaders must recognize the dangers of "Emotional Adultery." In Genesis 2:24, God established the foundation of a healthy marriage: *"Therefore a man shall leave his father and mother and be joined to his wife, and they shall become one flesh."*

The phrase "to be joined" does not just mean to be joined merely in the physical sense; it means that the man and his wife should be joined in every aspect of their being. They are to be joined physically, mentally, spiritually, and emotionally.

But, unfortunately, there are some men who are joining themselves emotionally to women other than their wives. In essence, they are committing "emotional adultery."

If you have any doubt that adultery can be committed on an emotional level, ask a wife who has been the victim of it. Most wives will readily admit that an adulterous affair occurs long before any physical contact takes place. They will contend that the husband committed "emotional adultery" first, which eventually led to physical adultery. Furthermore, many wives will say that the knowledge that their husband was emotionally intimate with another woman is even more painful than knowing that he had sexual relations with her.

What is "Emotional Adultery?" It is when one feels more emotionally connected to someone other than his or her own spouse. Brother, it is when your emotional needs are being met by someone other than your wife.

Every man has certain "emotional needs." First, there is "The Need for Significance." Every man needs to feel he is special and unique. He wants to know that God has gifted him for a significant purpose that he alone is suited to fulfill. Second, every man has "The Need for Success." This is the belief that he is achieving greatness—that he is successful and fulfilling the purpose God created him for. Thirdly, every man has "The Need for Respect." He needs to feel as though other people recognize him as a man of value and worth and appreciate the significance he has.

Brother, if these needs are being met by any woman other than your wife, then you are in an emotionally adulterous affair. When you want to be around another woman, talk to her, share personal things with her and pray with her more than you do with your own wife, you are having an emotional affair. If you look forward to seeing some sister in the church (even though you may not be sexually involved), you can't wait to be with her, talk to her, share something with her, you are committing emotional adultery. Do you think about another woman, obsess over her, and daydream about being with her? Do you anticipate seeing her, do you look for her in church or arrange your schedule to see her—if so, you are an emotional adulterer.

Of course, there are many reasons why a man will commit

emotional adultery. The excuses are boundless: "But you don't know what my wife is like. She doesn't understand or appreciate me; she doesn't respect me. But sister 'so and so'—she understands. I can talk to her. I tell her how I feel and what is bothering me. She encourages me and builds me up."

There will always be some woman who is glad to "build you up"—especially if you are a leader in the church. There is something very attractive about spiritual leadership and the anointing. People who are very needy and emotionally weakened are often drawn to it and enticed by the compassion spiritual leaders demonstrate. They will often say things like, "You are so wise, so anointed. You are such a compassionate and understanding pastor. I love to hear you preach. I'm your biggest fan. I've heard Benny Hinn and Reinhard Bonnke, but you are the best." But don't be naive. The wise and experienced leader will see it for what it is—a Proverbs 5:23 snare—a trap that captures foolish and undiscerning leaders.

Leaders beware, when you rely on another woman to provide you with the things your wife should be providing to you, you are committing emotional adultery. And take heed, emotional adultery is usually a precursor to physical adultery. Physical adultery doesn't "just happen." It occurs because a man and a woman first became emotionally connected and comfortable with each other.

AMNON AND TAMAR
AVOID SPIRITUAL ATTACHMENTS

"Then Amnon lay down and pretended to be ill; and when the king came to see him, Amnon said to the king, 'Please let Tamar my sister come and make a couple of cakes for me in my sight, that I may eat from her hand.' And David sent home to Tamar, saying, 'Now go to your brother Amnon's house, and prepare food for him.' Then Amnon said to Tamar, 'Bring the food into the

bedroom, that I may eat from your hand.' And Tamar took the cakes which she had made, and brought them to Amnon her brother in the bedroom. Now when she had brought them to him to eat, he took hold of her and said to her, 'Come, lie with me, my sister'" (2 Samuel 13:6-11).

Tamar was Amnon's sister. He should have loved her as a brother and protected her well-being, but instead he allowed lust to consume him and he abused her sexually. It is a tragedy that, unfortunately, is played out again and again in the church community between brothers and sisters in Christ.

Leaders must recognize the dangers of developing a spiritual intimacy with those of the opposite sex in church and ministry situations. It has been called "Spiritual Adultery" when one allows himself or herself to become intimately and inappropriately attached to someone on a spiritual level.

As stated, Genesis 2:24 instructs a man to be joined to his wife. Not only is this a "joining" in the physical and emotional sense, it also refers to their being joined spiritually. Husbands are to be joined, or cleave, to their wives spiritually. They are to pray together, to minister together, to identify prophetically together. Unfortunately, there are some men who are cleaving spiritually to women other than their wives. In essence, they are committing "spiritual adultery."

What is "spiritual adultery?" It is when one allows himself to become more spiritually compatible with a woman other than his own wife. It is when you seem to "connect" more "in the spirit" with some other woman. Maybe you have certain spiritual gifts—you are a prophet, an intercessor, a worship leader and this other woman shares the same gifts and spiritual passions. The two of you seem so plugged into each other spiritually.

But your wife, (sarcastically) she just isn't on the "same level" as you are spiritually. You try to tell her what you are seeing prophetically, or what God showed you in a dream, or in prayer—and all she cares about is reminding you to fix the car or pay the bills or watch the kids. She just isn't spiritual.

But sister "so and so"—she understands. She is in tune with what God is doing in you. She understands the prophetic word, or the "dream God gave you." She has the same burdens, the same insights. She prays for the same things and sees the same things—it is like God has given her to you as a "spiritual soul mate."

Ridiculous! There is only one woman you are to be joined with: your wife. Spiritual adultery occurs by joining yourself to another woman, being more spiritually intimate with her rather than your wife.

If you are spiritually plugged into another woman and not your wife, you are in danger and you need to repent. You better stop praying with that woman and go home and pray with your wife. Stop prophesying to that woman and start prophesying to your wife, talking to your wife, and interceding with your wife. Why? Because most adultery does not begin with a sexual encounter, most adultery begins at the spiritual and emotional level.

It is also important to note that most adultery committed by pastors and church leaders does not occur with a prostitute, or a stranger in a one night stand; most adultery occurs with women in the church. As noted from the above survey, among the respondent pastors who committed adultery, 69 percent came from within their own congregations, including 17 percent who were counselees.[10] It is also interesting to note that most men and women never intended to have an affair. They never expected, or began a relationship with the plan for it to end in adultery. Affairs occur because they allow themselves to be drawn into emotional, spiritual relationships with that persona that they should be having with their spouse.

If you are committing spiritual or emotional adultery, you must end that relationship immediately! Stop talking to that person, stop visiting that person, stop calling her—erase her number from your cell phone and if you happen to be in the same ministry as her, quit it immediately. If you are a pastor and she is in your church, you need to pull back completely. Keep your greetings short and sharp and withdraw from everything that encourages an emotional or spiritual intimacy between you.

Be firm and decisive! You don't need to explain it to her. You don't need to have a meeting and tell her why you are pulling back. Don't feel like she is entitled to an explanation; you don't owe her anything, nor are you obligated to say anything more to her. The only one you are obligated to is your own wife. So cut if off. No more conversations, no more prayer meetings, no more interaction whatsoever. "But what if she gets offended and leaves the church?" For your sake, the sake of your family, the sake of the church—and for her sake—that is probably the best thing.

DAVID AND BATHSHEBA
AVOID THE DANGERS OF AUTHORITY

"Then it happened one evening that David arose from his bed and walked on the roof of the king's house. And from the roof he saw a woman bathing, and the woman was very beautiful to behold. So David sent and inquired about the woman. And someone said, 'Is this not Bathsheba, the daughter of Eliam, the wife of Uriah the Hittite?' Then David sent messengers, and took her; and she came to him, and he lay with her, for she was cleansed from her impurity; and she returned to her house" (2 Samuel 11:2-4).

As king over Israel, David had unique access that only his

authority could give. His power, his influence was irresistible. Even if Bathsheba wanted to repel the king's advances, she had no chance against the sovereign command he had over her life and that of her family. Sadly, he used his position to bring Uriah's wife under his control and took advantage of her.

Leaders, whether they realize it or not, have a certain amount of influence over those who submit to their authority. This is especially true when the spiritual leader assumes the role of a counselor to those who are suffering or in need.

In fact, many of the people attending our churches are deeply troubled and emotionally wounded. They may be going through a divorce or suffering neglect in their marriage; they may be reeling from childhood trauma or working through issues of rejection and insecurity. As a result, many of these struggling saints are very needy; they may lack self-worth or are looking for affirmation and support. Many are broken hearted; they are lonely and afraid. And most are simply looking for a compassionate ear to listen to them and validate their pain.

As pastors, we are called to love these suffering souls with empathy and understanding. We need to guide them to the Healer who can mend their wounded spirits. However, as we minister to them, we need to be very cautious. There is a great danger here—a subtle snare—especially when the one coming to us for comfort is of the opposite sex.

Naturally, when she (or he) comes to you—the pastor—you listen. You show compassion, understanding, affirmation and love, the very things that she (or he) is in desperate need of. As a result, an unhealthy attachment can develop. She begins to regard you as a special person in her life: her source of empowerment, support and self-worth. She becomes emotionally dependent on you and—if you are not careful—she subconsciously begins to see you as her surrogate parent or spouse. Emotionally, you become the father or husband she has always longed for.

And if that's not bad enough, this dependence can affect you—the pastor—as well. It becomes very gratifying to know that you are so important, so needed and such a powerful force in someone's life. In fact, many pastors, who themselves are emotionally wounded and insecure, need to be needed. They need to know they are admired, respected, and appreciated. And it is especially gratifying when the one appreciating you is a younger, attractive member of the opposite sex.

It becomes even more gratifying when the pastor's emotional needs go unmet in his own marriage. If his wife continually nags, complains, and tears him down—if she often criticizes him and threatens his self-worth—then he too may develop a dependency on the counseling relationship. Not because he is receiving counsel, but because he is receiving what he needs emotionally: respect, affirmation, a sense of importance and self-worth—things that he cannot get anywhere else.

The result is an emotionally dependent pastor–parishioner relationship. It is an extremely dangerous snare. It is very often the beginning of an affair.

There are three rules that will deliver you from this snare.

First and foremost, love your spouse. The best defense against falling in love with a parishioner is to stay in love with your wife. Learn to appreciate the better qualities of your spouse, make an effort to talk with her and compliment her and express your affection. Remember that love grows through expression and dies with neglect. Proverbs 5:18-20 emphasizes this as well: *"...rejoice with the wife of your youth. As a loving deer and a graceful doe, let her breasts satisfy you at all times; and always be enraptured with her love. For why should you, my son, be enraptured by an immoral woman, and* be embraced in the arms of a seductress?"

Second, let the sisters counsel the sisters (and the brothers counsel the brothers). Titus 2:3-4 says, *"the older women...(should) admonish the young women."* The Apostle Paul understood human nature well when he told church leaders to stay away from those young women. *"If they need admonition or counsel,"* the wise apostle wrote, *"let the older, godly women take care of it."* Amen!

After a recent Sunday Morning service, I was in the church lobby greeting people as they departed the sanctuary. Suddenly, a young, attractive, blonde woman approached me. I had never met her before and greeted her as I do all new visitors. As we shook hands, she looked at me with tears in her eyes and said, "Your sermon really touched me today. I've been going through some really difficult times lately and..." She paused to wipe a tear from her eye with a handkerchief. "And I think you might be able to help me. Do you think we could meet together during the week and talk privately?"

At that moment, a million red flags went up in my head and warning sirens began to scream in my spirit. It was the Holy Ghost imprint on my character telling me, "Danger, danger—this is trouble! Don't do it." With that, I looked at her with sincere compassion in my eyes and said, "You know what I think you really need? You know what I think could really help you? We have some powerful, experienced, Holy Spirit-anointed sisters in our church. They are the wives of our deacons and elders and pastors; in fact, there is one right behind you. Let me introduce you to her. I know she would be glad to meet with you and talk and pray with you and..."

"No thanks." She said. Her eyes cleared up. The tremble in her voice disappeared. The hanky was stuffed into her purse. She thrust her chin up, brushed her hair out of her face and out the door she went. I never saw her again.

Did I offend her? Perhaps, but I take no chances with my integrity. Did I miss out on an opportunity to heal a hurting soul? Absolutely not. I offered her an opportunity to meet with some powerful, deeply wise and spiritual women. They would have ministered the grace and love of God to that lady in a way that no man could ever minister to her. Sadly, she rejected it.

Keep it short and simple. If you find that you absolutely must counsel with a woman, remember this acrostic: D-O-N'-T - K-I-S-S. Discuss Only (what you) Need To, Keep It Short (and) Simple. In other words, provide compassion and counsel but stay focused on the issue at hand. Refrain from offering the kind of support and sympathy that produces an emotional connection leading to a dependency. As well, keep the session short and simple. Avoid delving into issues and areas that are deep and intimate, emotionally volatile and require excessive amounts of time. If the counselee requires that kind of attention, refer him or her to a professional or a counselor of the same sex.

The *Baker Encyclopedia of Psychology and Counseling* suggests that the technique of "co-counseling" is often necessary in situations where a counselee could develop an unhealthy attachment to the counselor. It explains that therapists can reduce the transference of affection and emotional dependence coming from a counselee by the use of co-therapists. Using two counselors reduces the intensity of the patient's attachment by dispersing it among the two.[11] As much as possible, ministers should use the same approach by referring counselees of the opposite sex to his or her spouse, board member, or staff member.

Don't be intimidated by someone's neediness. Some people may try to manipulate you into investing more time and energy than you should. But being a pastor does not obligate you to being someone's personal counselor 24 hours a day, 7 days a week—especially with the opposite sex. A woman once complained to her pastor, "I need you to be there for me more often. I need you to check on me. I need to know I'm not alone." Wisely, he said, "I'm sorry, but I'm not going to do that. If you need some help, or advice, you can pick up the phone and call the office. I'm there, as well as other staff members. But don't expect me to meet all your needs."

SOLOMON AND HIS MANY FOREIGN WOMEN
STAYING PURE IN A WORLD OF CONCUBINES

"But King Solomon loved many foreign women, as well as the daughter of Pharaoh: women of the Moabites, Ammonites, Edomites, Sidonians, and Hittites—from the nations of whom the LORD had said to the children of Israel, 'You shall not intermarry with them, nor they with you. Surely they will turn away your hearts after their gods...' Solomon clung to these in love. And he had seven hundred wives, princesses, and three hundred concubines; and his wives turned away his heart" (1 Kings 11:1-3).

King Solomon was the most powerful man in the world leading the most powerful nation in the world. Israel was the reigning superpower and every surrounding country wanted to establish a treaty with them. Ironically, the way such treaties were forged was through marriage. Neighboring kings would offer their daughters in matrimony to seal a lifelong alliance; and for the king of the most powerful and richest nation in the world, offers of marriage were without end. Very often there would appear before Solomon's throne another foreign king with his beautiful young daughter offering her to him in marital alliance. Eventually, this unending supply of proposals, together with his own lust for women, resulted in 300 wives. Of course, marriage treaties were not the only way Solomon got his wives; the treaties simply awakened the monster of lust within. Almost every woman he was attracted to he took for himself, until he had a supply of 700 concubines. Promiscuity was ubiquitous and Solomon indulged it all.

Most people find it somewhat humorous that King Solomon could have such a harem, but is it not true that some men today have similar harems living in their minds. As it was for Solomon, promiscuity is ubiquitous today. We live in a culture of unlimited concubines. Our lives are inundated with offers of lust at every turn. Billboards, television, books, magazines and, of course, the Internet offer hundreds, if not thousands, of virtual concubines to move into the hearts and minds of willing men. And sadly, too many men—and pastors —are willing.

A survey by *Leadership Magazine* showed 40 percent of pastors regularly struggle with pornography.[12] Dr. Wayne Benson, former president of Emerge Ministries, reported that 28 percent of calls into their help line concerned some form of secret sexual sin and 20 percent were seeking help to overcome pornography.

Today, not only must we be careful of spiritual, emotional and physical adultery, we must be concerned about "virtual adultery." This is a sexual or romantic encounter that is virtual; it occurs online, via the Internet or some other means without the need for a physical partner. For men, it usually involves pornographic pictures or video, whereas women are more susceptible to email romances and social websites. Studies show that with unlimited, ubiquitous access to the Internet, virtual adultery is an unseen epidemic that is polluting untold millions of minds and destroying thousands of families.

More than we realize, men and woman are becoming addicted to virtual sex. Consider the following:
- Everyday 200 new pornography Web sites pop up.
- 75 percent of hits on the Web are looking for a porn site.
- The largest group of viewers of porn are boys between the age of 13 and 18 years old.
- Almost 90 percent of American teens view porn online.
- 94 percent of men have been exposed to pornography before the age of 20.[13]

The reality is no man can be faithful to his wife when there is a harem living in his mind. Imagine how Solomon's first wife felt when she discovered she would be sharing her husband with 299 more women, not mention the other 700 girlfriends. Ancient cultural norms or not, the damage this does to a woman's emotional well-being is incalculable.

Not only does it hurt the wife and the family, it devastates a ministry. How many churches have been ruined and congregations shattered because their pastor was a Solomon with a harem in his mind. Spiritual leaders must be honest with themselves and admit that lust exists in their heart. They must confess their sin to God and repent of any desire to act on the feelings they have. Remember the warnings of Proverbs 5, *"His own iniquities entrap the wicked man, and he is caught in the cords of his sin. He shall die for lack of instruction, and in the greatness of his folly he shall go astray."*

In some cases, prayer and repentance is not enough. Leaders who have a difficult time controlling their urges and actions may need to adopt a more aggressive plan for deliverance. Make yourself accountable to another leader or leaders. Confess your struggle to him or her and allow them the right to speak into your life and question you on a regular basis. Having an accountability group or partner is not a sign of weakness—it is a sign of strength. It reveals a depth of character that refuses to continue compromising one's integrity.

One study done at Dallas Theological Seminary examined 237 instances of Christians (mostly in leadership) who suffered moral failure. One interesting commonality was revealed: of the 237 men who fell, not one of them had accountability relationships with other men.[14] Perhaps the greatest safeguard we can have against the Solomon Syndrome is a willingness to take instruction and receive correction—in other words establish accountability partners. In Proverbs 5, we were introduced to a foolish man who was enraptured by a seductress, entrapped by his own iniquities, and caught in the cords of his own sin. However, Proverbs 5:12-13 gives additional insight to his mistake. He said, *"How I have hated instruction, and my heart despised correction! I have not obeyed the voice of my teachers, nor inclined my ear to those who instructed me!"* This man fell prey to adultery because he refused accountability; he refused to listen to the instructive warnings around him.

God will raise up voices to warn you. He loves you and cares about you; He cares about your marriage, your children and your church. God will do everything He can to keep you from falling into temptations. However, these warnings do not usually come from supernatural sources or heavenly visitations; more often they come from sources very close to us.

Warnings come from colleagues in ministry. As leaders, we often have blind spots that make it hard for us to see our own weaknesses. But when others look at us from different perspectives, they can identify where we are vulnerable. Colleagues in leadership, such as deacons, elders, and other pastors can often be more objective and emotionally detached than we who have invested so much in a situation. As such, they can more accurately discern the snares that we may be naively walking into.

If a colleague confronts or challenges you on a point of weakness, resist the tendency to become defensive and rigid or rationalize your behavior. Instead, make it a point to prayerfully consider the merit of their opinion. God may be using them to force our attention on areas that we have been ignoring the Spirit's call to. One way to "test" the warning is to share it with your spouse or another colleague, thus allowing another objective party to verify or refute it.

Warnings come from subordinates. Staff members who serve under us should not be expected to ignore our indiscretions, nor are they acting disloyal if they point them out. In fact, it is a demonstration of allegiance when a subordinate takes his leader aside and shares a concern.

If you are a subordinate, you should not have to "cover" for your leader's indiscretions. If you see areas of sin or compromise, for your leader's sake, and with humility and respect, confront him or her. If he or she does not hear you, then follow the directive of Matthew 18:15-17, *"Moreover if your brother sins against you, go and tell him his fault between you and him alone. If he hears you, you have gained your brother. But if he will not hear, take with you one or two more, that 'by the mouth of two or three witnesses every word may be established.' And if he refuses to hear them, tell it to the church. But if he refuses even to hear the church, let him be to you like a heathen and a tax collector."* First, bring another subordinate and confront him again. If he still refuses to hear you, bring it to other authorities in the church such as the deacons, elders, or other leadership council—which, in a sense, is the same as "telling it to the church."

Warnings come from your own spouse. The number one

defense God has given you to protect you from adultery is your wife or husband. Our spouses (especially the wives) have an uncanny ability to discern suspicious characters in the church, especially when it comes to threats to the marriage.

I have often found that my wife (and the wives of many leaders in my church) is, by nature, more discerning, intuitive and sensitive to the hidden motives of people's spirits. She will often say, "There is something about that person." Or "I think you should be more careful about that lady." I can honestly say that her accuracy in detecting wolves in the flock is uncanny.

Furthermore, I have dealt with numerous marriages where the husband has fallen in adultery. In almost every case, the wife discerned it long before the sin was exposed. The wife had sensed it even when her husband was worshiping God in church, serving in ministry, and telling everyone that his marriage was great.

If your spouse warns you about some brother or sister in the church, listen up. It could be that God has showed her or him something that you are blinded to.

A FINAL WARNING

Leaders, it doesn't matter how spiritual or successful one is. If a leader is careless regarding the opposite sex, he is setting himself up for trouble. Don't blame the devil. Don't blame loose women. Blame the man who has acted foolishly. Again, Proverbs 5:22-23 warns us: *"His own iniquities entrap the wicked man, and he is caught in the cords of his sin. He shall die for lack of instruction, and in the greatness of his folly he shall go astray."*

Leaders, we have been entrusted with a sacred duty—into our care has been committed the people of God. Let us bow before Him in true humility and confession. Having renounced those impure streams flowing in our hearts, let us remove from our lives everything that may snare us and determine to draw closer to Him each day. His promise of mercy and forgiveness will meet us there.

A FINAL WORD

Brethren, if a man is overtaken in any trespass, you who are spiritual restore such a one in a spirit of gentleness, considering yourself lest you also be tempted.

Galatians 6:1

Perhaps the greatest tragedy of Saul's story is that he never found a place of repentance and, consequently, never experienced healing and restoration. It's a sad indication of what happens to leaders who continue unabated in willful rebellion: eventually their sin will disqualify them from leadership and bring ruin to themselves, their families, their ministries and disgrace the Kingdom of God. To find a lesson on the healing and restoration of the leader, one most look beyond the life of Saul to that of his successor, David.

But can a church leader who has fallen and brought reproach on himself even be restored? It is a fair question and one many have asked based on the demands of Paul's letters to both Titus and Timothy. A leader must be "blameless."

A bishop then must be blameless, the husband of one wife, temperate, sober-minded, of good behavior, hospitable, able to teach... (1 Timothy 3:2)

But let these also first be tested; then let them serve as deacons, being found blameless. (1 Timothy 3:10)

For a bishop must be blameless, as a steward of God, not self-willed, not quick-tempered, not given to wine, not violent, not greedy for money... (Titus 1:7)

Obviously, the word "blameless" does not mean sinlessness or perfection. If that were the case no mortal would be qualified for Christian leadership. More accurately, the word implies being free from accusations of immorality with regard to reputation in the church and community. The question therefore is this: "Can a minister who has fallen in sin ever have his reputation restored to a position of integrity and moral trustworthiness?

In the opinion of this author, yes!

Paul makes this clear in Galatians 6:1: *"Brethren, if a man is overtaken in any trespass, you who are spiritual restore such a one in a spirit of gentleness, considering yourself lest you also be tempted."* The gospel is a message of forgiveness, redemption and restoration for the sinner. This was clearly demonstrated by Jesus after Peter publicly betrayed Him on three occasions (Mark 14:68-72). After the resurrection, Jesus did not reject Peter and disqualify him for leadership. On the contrary, Jesus tested the depth of his repentance and restored him to his apostleship (John 21:15-17).

Another example is found in Acts 15:37-40 concerning Mark. Paul refused him a place on his leadership team because of his failure. Later however, in 2 Timothy 4:11, Paul instructed Mark to be brought to him *"for he is useful to me for ministry."* Granted, Mark's failure was more an issue of cowardice than immorality, but the principle remains: leaders who fail can be restored once they prove their worthiness and regain trust.

This is good news, especially for the reader who sees himself in the example of Saul. Perhaps this book has caused you to recognize certain shortcomings and provided you with practical insight on correcting unhealthy behavior. In the event, however, you find yourself in that place of severe moral failure and public reproach and have been disqualified from leadership, the road back to restoration may be long and difficult, but not impossible.

Having served as a facilitator for the restoration of leaders who fell in sin, were removed from ministry and underwent a restoration process, I believe there are certain key factors that must be present in the restoration process:

The Need for Repentance: We are saved by grace, but not without repentance. God forgives our sin, but only after we turn from it. Acts 3:19 says *"Repent therefore and be converted, that your sins may be blotted out, so that times of refreshing may come from the presence of the Lord..."* Repentance is both inward and outward. It is inward in the sense that there is genuine grief over the sin and remorse for what has been done. It is also external in that one's conduct, lifestyle and environment indicate a change of direction. Essentially, repentance demonstrates that one deeply regrets what was done and has made every indication to prevent doing it again.

The Need for Discipline: Solomon wrote in Ecclesiastes 8:11: *"Because the sentence against an evil work is not executed speedily, therefore the heart of the sons of men is fully set in them to do evil."* When a leader breaks the trust given to him by his followers and the organization that endorsed him, there must be punitive action. Yes, there should be a place for grace, but that comes after repentance has been shown and justice has been satisfied. We are moral beings, created in the image of God who gave us a sense of morality and righteousness. For an offender to be forgiven and restored without any tangible consequence violates our natural sense of justice. We cannot trust that the offender has "learned his lesson" unless we know he has been disciplined—even punished for his offense.

The Need for Time: Most people are not against

restoration; they are against quick restoration. The passage of time is required. There are many levels of emotional pain, family dysfunction and spiritual brokenness through which the fallen leader must go before he (and his spouse and family) can be effective in leadership once again. Each of these stages cannot be experienced in a short amount of time; there are often deep, underlying issues that enabled sin which must come to the surface and be dealt with. Most of these phases take several years or longer. It's similar to a person who has a knife wound. We can pull the knife out right away, but there must be time for the wound to heal. And the deeper the wound, the longer it takes to heal. Without proper time, the wound is likely to fester and lead to other crippling issues.

The Need for Rehabilitation: Unfortunately, some leaders who fall and seek restoration, find the term "rehabilitation" distasteful. They equate it with being an addict or someone who is emotionally dysfunctional—not how they like to think of themselves. The reality is, however, that "rehabilitation" is exactly what is needed to properly restore a leader. After his sin with Bathsheba, David wrote, *"Create in me a clean heart, O God, and renew a steadfast spirit within me."* (Psalm 51:10) Essentially, David acknowledge his need for deep, internal change. This is the work of rehabilitation. It deals with the core drivers, the triggers, the patterns and heart issues that enabled the sin in the first place while training the leader in new, healthy ways to respond to the causes and effects of his sin.

The Need for Supportive Accountability: Accountability is an essential component of the restoration process. If the fallen leader could restore himself on his own, he would not have fallen in the first place. On the contrary, he has already demonstrated that such freedom without accountability will result in the abuse of privacy. This is why, in Galatians 6:1, Paul instructed: *"Brethren, if a man is overtaken in any trespass,* *you who are spiritual restore such a one..."* It implies that the restoration process is superintended by others who are spiritual, which could also mean spiritual authorities. Accountability implies "answer-ability." In other words, the one being restored must be willing to answer for his daily behavior and be subject to probing questions. An important point however: Paul states that this must be done is a *"in a spirit of gentleness."* Those providing accountability must be careful to demonstrate compassion and communicate a supportive concern for the one being restored.

The Need for Evaluation: Every denomination has an ordination process. Candidates are reviewed and approved for ordination having demonstrated the credibility required to be entrusted with ministerial authority. It is not that the denomination ordains to ministry, only God can do that. Rather, the ordaining body serves to validate the call from God that the candidate claims to have. A similar process of review and approval must also be employed for one seeking restoration to leadership. Having completed the rehabilitation process, he must be willing to pass before a review board who evaluates reports generated by his accountability team, interviews him and determines if he is once again trustworthy. Ultimately, it is this body that provides the endorsement that the candidate is above reproach and blameless having fulfilled the requirements of restoration.

More and more we are hearing about leaders who have fallen into sin. Mostly, these are not bad men or women; more typically, they are good people struggling to deal with issues of unhealth. Rarely does a leader fall maliciously, with intent to hurt people or the organization he is leading. Usually, they have simply lost control of their own impulse and were overcome by sin.

Restoration is not an easy process. In fact, it can be very hard and humiliating. It will try the inner regions of one's true character like nothing else. But the man or woman who will submit to the process outlined above can be restored with even stronger character, deeper integrity and a greater awareness of the grace and power of God. Ultimately, this is the goal of restoration, not just the restoration to a position, but the restoration of character, healthy relationships and vibrant life in Jesus Christ.

ENDNOTES

Lesson Three
1. See article at BBC NEWS: http://news.bbc.co.uk/go/pr/fr/-/2/hi/africa/6294666.stm
2. See article at BBC NEWS: http://news.bbc.co.uk/go/pr/fr/-/2/hi/africa/5083534.stm
3. See article at BBC NEWS: http://news.bbc.co.uk/go/pr/fr/-/2/hi/africa/3672805.stm
4. See article at BBC NEWS: http://news.bbc.co.uk/go/pr/fr/-/2/hi/africa/6294666.stm
5. Jim Collins describes the chapter entitled: Level 5 Leadership. *Good to Great*, (New York, Harper Collins, 2001), page 17

Lesson Four
1. J. Oswald Sanders, *Spiritual Leadership*, (Chicago, Moody Press, 1994), page 53
2. See article at http://www.buildingchurchleaders.com/articles/2005/062905.html
3. Charles Colson, "Welcome to McChurch," *Christianity Today*, 9 November 1992, 33-35

Lesson Five
1. See article at http://en.wikipedia.org/wiki/Washington_Monument
2. See article at http://en.wikipedia.org/wiki/Washington_Monument.
3. Quote from Mark Driscoll; visit http://www.theelephantroom.com/2011/11/08/top-ten-quotes-from-elephant-room-1-and-another-twitter-contest/

Lesson Six
1. Julian Watkins "The 100 Greatest Advertisements" Moore Pub. Co, January 01, 1949
2. Various historians have claimed that this ad was placed, although they do not all agree on when or which newspaper, No one has yet been able to locate the original newspaper clipping. For more information, see article at http://www.antarctic-circle.org/advert.htm; Accessed February 27, 2006
3. Julian Watkins "The 100 Greatest Advertisements" Moore Pub. Co, January 01, 1949
4. By August 1, 1914, Shackleton and his crew of twenty six men set out from London for the frigid Antarctic. Unfortunately the expedition's goal had to be abandoned when their ship The Endurance was trapped and crushed by ice. Thereafter, Shackleton and his crew endured a grueling twenty two month journey by sledge across the frozen arctic. Miraculously—and hailed as a credit to Shackleton's leadership, every member of his crew survived the ordeal. What should have been a tragic failure has been hailed by history as a monument to exceptional leadership.
5. From CBS News online, Writing For Ronald Reagan, New York, Aug. 5, 2003 http://www.cbsnews.com/stories/2003/07/30/earlyshow/leisure/books/main565830.shtml; Accessed February 27, 2006
6. Bruce Wilkinson, *The Prayer of Jabez*, (Sisters, Oregon, Multnomah Publishers, 2000), page 47
7. See article at http://online.wsj.com/article/SB10001424052748704256604575294913333857770.html

Lesson Seven
1. See article at http://en.wikipedia.org/wiki/Billy_Graham
2. Richard Langford, "How to Empower Second Chair Leaders," *Leadership Teaching Magazine,* Vol. 6, Issue 1; Winter 2009; page 12

Lesson Eight
1. Gregg T. Johnson, *Crisis, Conflict and Change,* (Holmes NY, Global Leadership Training, 2010) page 83
2. See article at http://enrichmentjournal.ag.org/199804/086_managing_conflict_3.cfm (by Dr. Richard Dobbins)
3. Ron Susek, *Firestorm, Preventing and Overcoming Church Conflict (*Grand Rapids MI, Baker Book House) page 12
4. *Building Church Leaders*, published by Leadership Journal, 1998 Christianity Today, page 6.1

Lesson Nine
1. Gregg T. Johnson, *The Character of Leadership*, (Holmes NY, Global Leadership Training, 2003) page 18
2. See article at http://www.familysafemedia.com/pornography_statistics.html
3. 2000 survey (564 respondents) by *Leadership Magazine*: Pastors and Internet Pornography, Winter 2001, page 89
4. Michael Josephson; *Making Ethical Decisions* (Josephson Institute of Ethics; 2002 ed edition, March 2002)

Lesson Ten
1. 2000 survey (564 respondents) by *Leadership Magazine*: Pastors and Internet Pornography, Winter 2001, page 89
2. H. B. London, Jr., and Neil B. Wiseman, *Pastors at Risk*, Wheaton: Victor, 1993, page 22
3. Joe E. Trull and James E. Carter, "*Ministerial Ethics: Being a Good Minister in a Not -So-Good World*" (Nashville: Broadman and Holman, 1993) page 81
4. Wayne Goodall, "*Why Great Men Fall*"; New Leaf Press, Green Forest, Arizona; May 2005, page 12 (quoting Shirley Glass, "Not Just Friends")
5. J. Holroyd and A. Brodsky, "Does *Touching Patients Lead to Sexual Intercourse?*" Journal of Professional Psychology: Research and Practice (1980), pages 807–811
6. R. Folman, "*Therapist-Patient Sex: Attraction and Boundary Problems*," Psychotherapy (1991), pages 168–173.
7. 1998 Leadership poll surveyed nearly a thousand pastors (30 percent response rate) and equivalent number of non-subscribers to Christianity Today magazine.
8. http://www.ag.org/top/enrichment/pasgrw_ethic_sexualethics.cfm
9. Gary Collins, *Excellence and Ethics in Counseling* (Dallas, Tex.: Word, 1991) page 67
10. 1998 Leadership poll surveyed nearly a thousand pastors (30 percent response rate) and equivalent number of non-subscribers to Christianity Today magazine.
11. D. Benner, ed., *Baker Encyclopedia of Psychology and Counseling* (Grand Rapids: Baker, 1985) page 242
12. 2000 survey (564 respondents) by *Leadership Magazine*: Pastors and Internet Pornography, Winter 2001, page 89
13. Wayne Goodall, "*Why Great Men Fall*"; New Leaf Press, Green Forest, Arizona; May 2005, page 57
14. Ibid, page 58

ABOUT THE AUTHOR

Gregg T. Johnson is Lead Pastor of The Mission Church in New York State, founder of Global Leadership Training and Managing Editor of *Leadership Teaching Magazine*. Pastor Gregg is ordained with The Assemblies of God, serves as a New York District Presbyter overseeing the AG Hudson Valley Section and lives in New York. He and his wife Laura have four sons, one daughter who is married, and two grandsons.

Entering full time ministry in 1984, Pastor Gregg has been preaching God's Word with a special gift for training leaders. His ministry at The Mission Church began in 1989 where he presently pastors. Under his leadership, the church continues to grow both in attendance and in leadership development, as well as in the expansion of its facilities.

Pastor Gregg is also founder and keynote speaker of Global Leadership Training, an international equipping ministry that provides leadership training conferences to pastors and church leaders in developing nations. Rather than centering on hype and sensationalism, these conferences provide practical teaching on character development and ministry management. Thousands of leaders have been enriched by Global Leadership Training and Pastor Gregg's ministry in the U.S., Canada, East Africa, West Africa, and India.

Gregg Johnson has authored four books: **The Character of Leadership, Raising the Standard of Leadership, Ethics for Church Leaders,** and **Crisis, Conflict and Change.** As well, he and his ministry staff publish **Leadership Teaching Magazine**, a 24-page quarterly periodical which addresses important topics on leadership and ministry and is provided to thousands of church leaders in developing countries.

Pastor Gregg's greatest passion is teaching and preaching the Word of God. He communicates the deep truths of Scripture with an energetic and prophetic passion in a way that is practical, inspirational, and life giving.

For more information contact:

The Mission Church
4101 Rt. 52
Holmes, NY 12531
www.missionchurch.com

Or visit him online at
www.GreggTJohnson.com
www.GlobalLeadershipTraining.org
www.LeadershipTeachingMagazine.com

OTHER BOOKS BY GREGG JOHNSON

Leadership will destroy the man whose character is not prepared for it. ***The Character of Leadership*** reveals the six pillars of a leader's character that provide a sturdy foundation to keep the leader secure through the pressures of promotion and

Lawyers have them, doctors have them, even civil authorities have them. But many church leaders, in an effort to grow their churches or enlarge their ministries, have violated principles of sound ethics. ***Ethics for Church Leaders*** provides a practical approach toward proper ministry protocols.

Crisis, Conflict and Change is an in-depth look at the challenges of leadership and leaders can actually transform difficult seasons into forward momentum which strengthen unity, enhance vision and grow the organization. A must read for all leaders!

From the pastor's family to his prayer life, from his preaching and worship to his fund raising practices, ***Raising the Standard*** exposes the troubling trends undermining today's leaders while calling them to a higher level of integrity and intensity.

LEADERSHIP TEACHING MAGAZINE

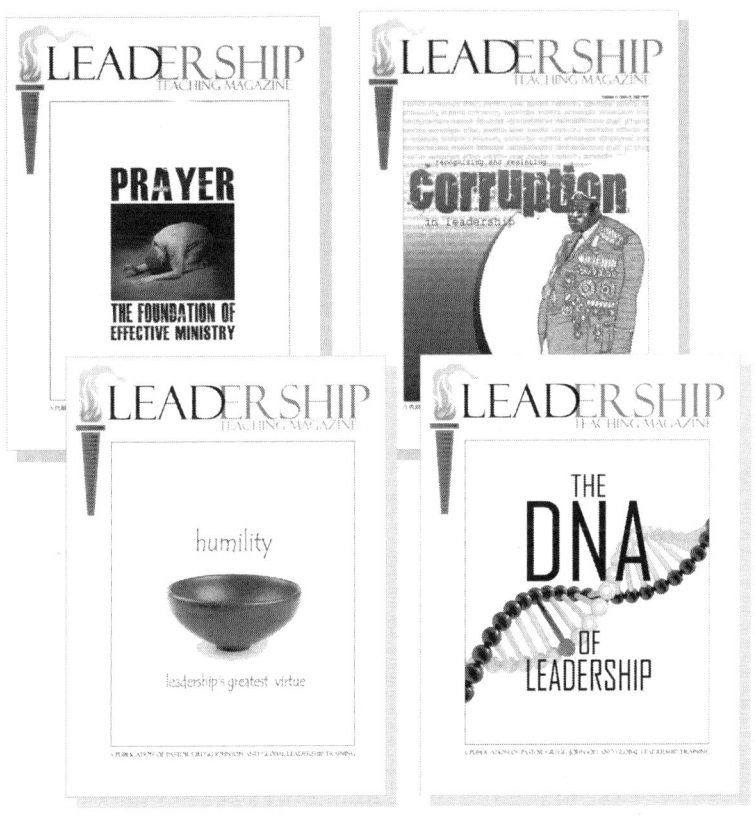

Leadership Teaching Magazine is a quarterly publication published by Gregg Johnson and Global Leadership Training. Each issue addresses a specific topic relevant to effective church leadership: finances, marriage and family, conflict, preaching, missions and much more. It is provided to thousands of pastors and church leaders around the world. For a free subscription, go to:

www.LeadershipTeachingMagazine.com